Pearl Harbor

Other titles in the series include:

Ancient Egypt
Ancient Greece
Ancient Rome
Elizabethan England
The Black Death
The Decade of the 2000s
The Digital Age
The Holocaust
The Early Middle Ages
The Late Middle Ages
The Renaissance

Pearl Harbor

Adam Woog

Bruno Leone
Series Consultant

San Diego, CA

Printed in the United States

For more information, contact:
ReferencePoint Press, Inc.
PO Box 27779
San Diego, CA 92198
www. ReferencePointPress.com

LIBRARY OF CONGRESS CATALOGING-IN-PUBLICATION DATA

Woog, Adam, 1953-
Pearl Harbor / by Adam Woog.
p. cm. -- (Understanding World history)
Includes bibliographical references and index.
ISBN-13: 978-1-60152-486-7 (hardback : alk. paper)
ISBN-10: 1-60152-486-2 (hardback : alk. paper)
1. Pearl Harbor (Hawaii), Attack on, 1941--Juvenile literature. 2. World War, 1939-1945--Causes--Juvenile literature. I. Title.
D767.92.W636 2013
940.54'26693--dc23

2012027684

Contents

Foreword

When the Puritans first emigrated from England to America in 1630, they believed that their journey was blessed by a covenant between themselves and God. By the terms of that covenant they agreed to establish a community in the New World dedicated to what they believed was the true Christian faith. God, in turn, would reward their fidelity by making certain that they and their descendants would always experience his protection and enjoy material prosperity. Moreover, the Lord guaranteed that their land would be seen as a shining beacon—or in their words, a "city upon a hill,"—which the rest of the world would view with admiration and respect. By embracing this notion that God could and would shower his favor and special blessings upon them, the Puritans were adopting the providential philosophy of history—meaning that history is the unfolding of a plan established or guided by a higher intelligence.

The concept of intercession by a divine power is only one of many explanations of the driving forces of world history. Historians and philosophers alike have subscribed to numerous other ideas. For example, the ancient Greeks and Romans argued that history is cyclical. Nations and civilizations, according to these ancients of the Western world, rise and fall in unpredictable cycles; the only certainty is that these cycles will persist throughout an endless future. The German historian Oswald Spengler (1880–1936) echoed the ancients to some degree in his controversial study *The Decline of the West.* Spengler asserted that all civilizations inevitably pass through stages comparable to the life span of a person: childhood, youth, adulthood, old age, and, eventually, death. As the title of his work implies, Western civilization is currently entering its final stage.

Joining those who see purpose and direction in history are thinkers who completely reject the idea of meaning or certainty. Rather, they reason that since there are far too many random and unseen factors at work on the earth, historians would be unwise to endorse historical predictability of any type. Warfare (both nuclear and conventional), plagues, earthquakes, tsunamis, meteor showers, and other catastrophic world-changing events have loomed large throughout history and prehistory. In his essay "A Free Man's Worship," philosopher and mathematician Bertrand Russell (1872–1970) supported this argument, which many refer to as the nihilist or chaos theory of history. According to Russell, history follows no preordained path. Rather, the earth itself and all life on earth resulted from, as Russell describes it, an "accidental collocation of atoms." Based on this premise, he pessimistically concluded that all human achievement will eventually be "buried beneath the debris of a universe in ruins."

Whether history does or does not have an underlying purpose, historians, journalists, and countless others have nonetheless left behind a record of human activity tracing back nearly 6,000 years. From the dawn of the great ancient Near Eastern civilizations of Mesopotamia and Egypt to the modern economic and military behemoths China and the United States, humanity's deeds and misdeeds have been and continue to be monitored and recorded. The distinguished British scholar Arnold Toynbee (1889–1975), in his widely acclaimed twelve-volume work entitled *A Study of History,* studied twenty-one different civilizations that have passed through history's pages. He noted with certainty that others would follow.

In the final analysis, the academic and journalistic worlds mostly regard history as a record and explanation of past events. From a more practical perspective, history represents a sequence of building blocks—cultural, technological, military, and political—ready to be utilized and enhanced or maligned and perverted by the present. What that means is that all societies—whether advanced civilizations or preliterate tribal cultures—leave a legacy for succeeding generations to either embrace or disregard.

Recognizing the richness and fullness of history, the ReferencePoint Press Understanding World History series fosters an evaluation and interpretation of history and its influence on later generations. Each volume in the series approaches its subject chronologically and topically, with specific focus on nations, periods, or pivotal events. Primary and secondary source quotations are included, along with complete source notes and suggestions for further research.

Moreover, the series reflects the truism that the key to understanding the present frequently lies in the past. With that in mind, each series title concludes with a legacy chapter that highlights the bonds between past and present and, more important, demonstrates that world history is a continuum of peoples and ideas, sometimes hidden but there nonetheless, waiting to be discovered by those who choose to look.

Important Events in the Attack on Pearl Harbor

1904
Japan attacks Russian naval vessels in China and Korea, triggering the Russo-Japanese war.

1905
Japan's victory in the Russo-Japanese War encourages expansion of the Japanese Empire.

1931
The Mukden (Manchuria) Incident sparks Japan's annexation of part of China.

1933
Japan resigns from the League of Nations after the organization condemns Japan's actions in China.

1934
Adolf Hitler becomes the leader of Germany.

1937
Japan's invasion of China results in full-blown conflict, the Second Sino-Japanese War; Japan fires on the USS *Panay* on the Yangtze River.

1939
The Nazis invade Poland, and war is declared between the Allied forces (led by England and France) and Nazi forces.

1900 / 1929 1934 1939

1940
Japan announces formation of the Greater East Asia Co-Prosperity Sphere; Japan, Germany, and Italy sign the Tripartite Pact.

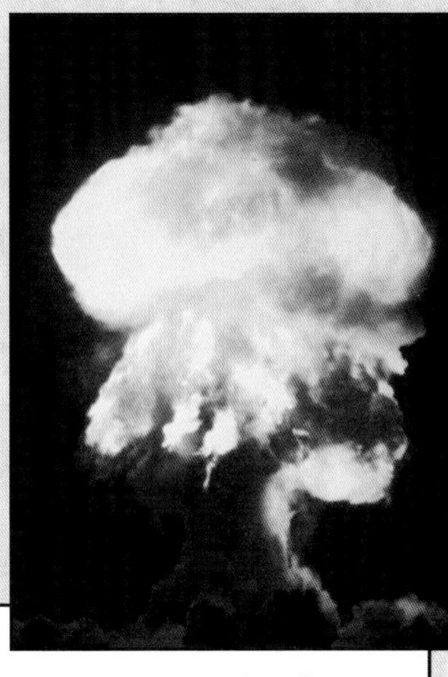

1942
The Battle of Midway marks a turning point in the Pacific war, as the United States begins to overcome Japanese military forces.

1943
The Battle of Stalingrad, a milestone in the European war, ends as the Soviet Union successfully thwarts Nazi invasion; Italy surrenders.

1945
Germany surrenders to Allied forces in Europe; after American atomic bombs destroy the cities of Hiroshima and Nagasaki, Japan announces its surrender, marking the end of the war.

1956
Japan joins the United Nations.

1940 1945 1950 1955 1960

1951
General Douglas MacArthur resigns as the head of the US occupation forces in Japan.

1952
America's occupation of Japan ends; the Treaty of San Francisco goes into effect, formally ending the war between Japan and forty-eight nations, including the United States.

1944
The Battle of Leyte Gulf, the largest naval battle of World War II, is the first instance of organized attacks by Japanese kamikaze (suicide) aircraft; the Battle of the Bulge marks a turning point in the Allies' successful dominance of the Nazis.

1941
After diplomatic talks between Japan and the United States formally end, Japanese forces carry out their surprise attack on Pearl Harbor; the United States declares war on Japan and shortly after that on Germany and Italy, marking America's entry into World War II.

Introduction

Pearl Harbor's Place in World History

Oahu, the main island of Hawaii, is the home of a large US naval base called Pearl Harbor. Today Pearl Harbor is one of the navy's busiest harbors. Combined with an adjacent air force facility, they form Joint Base Pearl Harbor-Hickam. But the name *Pearl Harbor* has special meaning beyond simply being a military base in a tropical paradise. The name immediately conjures up one particular event and one fateful day. The event was a surprise attack on the base by Japanese military forces, and the day was December 7, 1941.

Infamy

In the words of President Franklin D. Roosevelt, December 7 was "a date which will live in infamy."[1] It is one of the most important moments in modern history, both for America and the world. It was a turning point in World War II, which had been raging in Europe since 1939. Japan's shocking attack on Pearl Harbor sparked America's entry into the war, turning a relatively contained conflict into a true world war and altering the dynamics between the two sides. The vast raw resources, manufacturing capabilities, and manpower of the United States—coupled with those of its partners—made the Allies into a formidable, united, and ultimately victorious foe.

Prior to December 7 the war had been confined to Europe and North Africa. It pitted the Allies, a union of nations led by the United

Kingdom, against the Axis forces, led by Nazi Germany and Fascist Italy, as the Axis powers sought to invade the nations of Europe and beyond. Germany and Italy were already aligned with Japan, which shared their plans to expand, through force, the lands they controlled. In the case of the Empire of Japan, it sought to invade and occupy territory in eastern Asia and across the Pacific Ocean.

For years Japan's expansionist policy had created growing hostility between it and the Western nations with territorial interests in the Pacific: the United Kingdom, France, Netherlands, and especially the United States. These interests were largely economic. The Pacific territories provided valuable raw materials such as rubber and oil. Japan coveted—and desperately needed—these same raw materials. The events of December 7 brought the simmering hostility between the two sides to the boiling point. One day after the attack on Pearl Harbor, the United States declared war on Japan, and three days after that, it declared war on the other Axis powers. World War II thus spread from the European continent to the Pacific theater of war (to use a military term), creating a single, huge, cataclysmic struggle. Historian H.P. Willmott writes that Pearl Harbor "combined two very separate wars [into] one world war, the most terrible and costly war in history."[2]

The Repercussions of the War

The costs were indeed staggering. It is impossible to accurately measure casualties, but estimates put the total number at an estimated 60 million. And the economic losses were similarly devastating.

More broadly, the end of the long conflict led to significant changes in world politics. Notably, it resulted in the formation of the United Nations, the most important organization in the world devoted to international peace and cooperation. It also led to changes in Japan. For example, that nation had previously been a monarchy ruled by an emperor who was considered semidivine and was descended from centuries-old royalty. After Japan's defeat and the resulting American occupation, Japan replaced its feudal government with a Western-style democracy.

Furthermore, America's awakening as a world power in the aftermath of the attack on Pearl Harbor created a new balance of powers in global politics. Two superpower nations emerged from the war: the United States and the Soviet Union. These two nations had deeply different political and social philosophies. The United States was a democratic republic, whereas the Soviet Union was a Communist dictatorship. This division led to long-standing hostility between them and the

Sailors in a small craft rescue a survivor beside the sunken battleship USS West Virginia *on December 7, 1941. The Japanese attack on Pearl Harbor destroyed dozens of ships and aircraft and killed or injured thousands of US military personnel. It also pushed the United States into World War II.*

development of what came to be known as the Cold War. With varying degrees of intensity, the Cold War lasted from the end of World War II until the collapse of the Soviet Union in 1991. Willmott writes that December 7 "was the moment when . . . the United States of America was forced to assume the responsibilities of power and began to tread the road that, very shortly, would lead her into her inheritance as the greatest power in the world."[3] In short, December 7, 1941, resulted in a conflict that changed the world forever.

Chapter 1

What Led to the Attack on Pearl Harbor?

The attack on Pearl Harbor had deep roots that stretched back decades. A number of social, political, and economic factors formed a prelude to the assault. One of these was a rising sense of nationalism on the part of Japan, a conviction that the nation was destined for great things—specifically, to expand its holdings and be the dominant power in eastern Asia.

A sense of superiority was nothing new in Japan (or in many other countries, for that matter). But in the early decades of the twentieth century, the nation's sense of its destiny mushroomed. This was fostered, in large part, by Japan's military leaders, who increasingly dominated the government. Another group that passionately encouraged this view was the royal and aristocratic element in the country. They had an increasing influence over Japan's royal leader, Emperor Meiji, who was the absolute ruler of Japan and was considered by his people to be a semidivine figure who could do no wrong. All of these groups were supported by a number of ultranationalist, semimilitary organizations, such as the Black Dragon Society. This secretive and often ruthless organization's mission statement included an assertion that Japan needed to "check the expansion of the western powers [and] then to lay the foundation for a grand continental enterprise."[4]

All of the groups encouraged a belief in the importance of ethnic purity and a revival of Bushido, the ancient code of honor, bravery, and service that samurai warriors had once pledged. They particularly stressed two aspects of the Bushido tradition: the nobility of warfare and the virtue of self-sacrifice—including death—in the service of a master. They further believed that Japan had the military technology and the passion to overcome any resistance. Historian Janis Mimura writes, "Japanese [military leaders] remained exceedingly optimistic about their country's prospects for war and empire. . . . They believed that more than Japan's material resources, its human resources, namely the patriotic spirit, courage, discipline, and creativity of its people, were the fount of national strength."[5]

Victory over Russia

Historians point to several events that could be considered the beginning of nationalism in Japan. The most widely accepted of these is the Russo-Japanese War, a conflict from 1904 to 1905 with another realm that had powerful dreams of territorial domination: the vast Russian Empire. The dispute was over regions strategic to both sides, notably portions of the Korean Peninsula and Manchuria, a huge area bordered by China, Russia, and Korea. (It is now part of the People's Republic of China.) Both sides were especially keen to establish a naval base at Manchuria's Port Arthur (now Port Lüshun) west of the Korean Peninsula.

Early in 1904 Japan made the first move. It began the war by launching surprise attacks on Russian naval vessels stationed in Port Arthur and the Korean port of Chemulpo. Russia's royal leader, Czar Nicholas, enthusiastically endorsed retaliatory actions. He believed that his empire would quickly prevail in the ensuing war. In his opinion, Japan could not sustain a prolonged conflict. But the war, unpopular among the Russian people, proved to be a huge drain on Russia's treasury. Increasingly pressured to bring an end to the conflict, in 1905 Nicholas accepted US president Theodore Roosevelt's offer to mediate a peace settlement. This settlement strongly favored Japan. Notably, the Russian Empire essentially acknowledged Japanese control of Port Arthur, Korea, and some of the islands between the two countries—an event that encouraged Japan to continue its aggression in the region.

Japanese Expansion 1895–1938

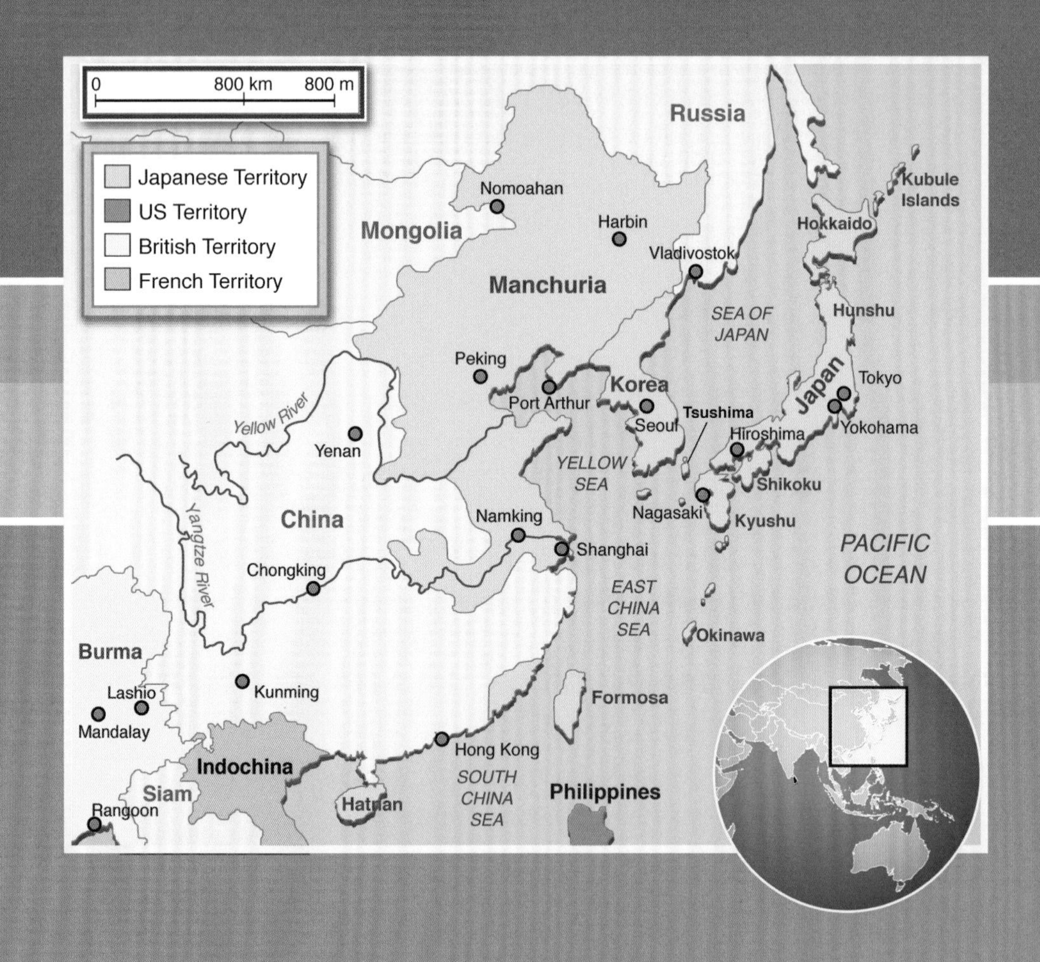

Japan's victory was a dramatic turning point in its history. The war launched the nation, which previously had been a minor player in global politics, into a role as the dominant military power in eastern Asia. Emboldened, Japan's military and political leaders intensified their expansionist plans and approved an escalating series of war budgets. They also drew up plans targeting more territories in eastern Asia and the Pacific, particularly those controlled by Western nations. These regions included Netherlands' Dutch East Indies (today Indonesia) as well as the British possessions of Malaya (today Malaysia), Hong Kong, Borneo, and India. Also among the targeted regions were French Indochina (modern-day Vietnam, Laos, and Cambodia), and Hawaii and the Philippines (which were then controlled by the United States).

Economic Factors

Economic need combined with a growing sense of nationalism fueled Japan's ambitious plans. By the 1920s Japan was a world leader in manufacturing, primarily because it had been neutral during World War I (1914–1918) and so had been barely touched by the devastations the conflict created. Compared with the severely crippled manufacturing facilities, resources, and treasuries of the European nations that had fought in the war, Japan's industry and trade were robust. Despite its strength in this area, Japan faced serious problems. For one thing, the government was encouraging growth in the nation's population. This growth, it felt, would justify Japan's need for expansion and also create a larger pool of soldiers and workers. Thanks to an intense campaign for larger families, Japan experienced a startling population explosion during this period. By 1930 there were so many Japanese people in the small island nation that the country could not grow enough food or manufacture enough goods for itself. At the same time, the government established high taxes on imported goods in an effort to make the country self-sufficient. But the combination backfired, crippling the nation's ability to sustain itself.

Adding to Japan's economic problems—and its expansionist goals—were those related to the business organizations called *zaibatsu*. The *zaibatsu* were the nation's huge trading and manufacturing conglomerates. As was true of businesses around the world, throughout the 1930s the *zaibatsu* fought to survive in the face of a global economic crisis known as the Great Depression. The *zaibatsu* were naturally eager to prosper and expand their businesses, so they strongly supported the government's territorial plans.

There was another crucial point: Japan was a small island nation with very limited land that was usable for agriculture or factory expansion. As a result, it had virtually no natural resources or raw materials. Specifically, it needed to import vast quantities of iron, rubber, and oil to support its manufacturing facilities, as well as food for its growing population. Japan's leaders were keenly aware of the abundance of these materials elsewhere in Asia.

The obvious answer was colonial expansion. Occupying portions of eastern Asia would allow large numbers of Japan's residents to migrate and relieve its overcrowding. The new colonies would also serve as sources of raw materials and food, as well as provide markets for the manufactured goods that Japan produced. And so the plans for expansion rapidly increased. Historian John W. Dower comments, "As the world plunged into depression and instability, the country's leaders responded (and contributed) to this disorder with an increasingly frantic quest for control over the markets and resources of Asia."[6]

The Manchurian Invasion

By 1930 Japan's leaders had set their sights on annexing one region in particular: Manchuria, where the Russo-Japanese War had begun. But they needed a pretext to invade—that is, they had to find something that would justify their actions to the outside world. So in the fall of 1931, agents of the Imperial Japanese Army deliberately triggered an episode called the Mukden Incident (also called the Manchurian Incident). In this incident military officers arranged for a small explosion to occur close to a railroad line. This line was operated by a Japanese company that had taken it over from Russia. The explosion, by itself, was minor and caused no significant damage. However, the Japanese military, blaming it on Chinese dissidents, used the event as an excuse to launch a full invasion.

The Japanese forces that swarmed into the region quickly overran the poorly equipped Chinese military, and within six months Japan controlled all of Manchuria. It "freed" the native Manchu people, an ethnic minority, from Chinese rule and created a puppet state—that is, a region that was officially independent and self-governed, but that in practice was controlled from the outside. Manchuria was essentially

The Greater East Asia Co-Prosperity Sphere

In 1940 Japan announced the formation of the Greater East Asia Co-Prosperity Sphere. This organization was designed to unite the nations of eastern Asia for mutual good. It promised economic, political and social independence, but it was actually a mechanism through which Japan could turn these countries into colonies under its control. The official statement made in June 1940 at the formation of the organization read, in part:

> The world stands at a great historic turning point, and it is about to witness the creation of new forms of government, economy, and culture, based upon the growth and development of sundry groups of states. Japan, too, is confronted by a great trial such as she has never experienced in history. In order to carry out fully at this juncture our national policy in accordance with the lofty spirit in which the country was founded, it is an important task of urgent necessity to us that we should grasp the inevitable trends in the developments of world history, effect speedily fundamental renovations along all lines of government, and strive for the perfection of a state structure for national defense.

WW2Timelines.com, "The Greater East Asia Co-Prosperity Sphere: The Official Statement of the Japanese Government, August 1, 1940," 2011. ww2timelines.com.

now a Japanese colony. Renaming it Manchukuo, the Japanese began using it as a rich source of raw materials for export to Japan.

Japan's annexation of Manchuria was strongly condemned by other nations. A number of them broke off diplomatic relations in protest. Furthermore, China persuaded the member countries of the League of Nations (the predecessor of the United Nations) to avoid recognizing Manchukuo as a legitimate government. Japan used this largely symbolic action as an excuse to resign from the organization. This was a step forward in Japan's expansionist plans. It was now free to ignore the league's charter, which laid out international rules of conduct that stressed peaceful negotiation over aggression.

Japan followed its annexation of Manchuria with an invasion that drove farther into China, notably into Inner Mongolia. The army that resisted Japan, called the Nationalists and led by Chiang Kai-shek, was forced to steadily withdraw inland as Japan invaded from the coast. Chiang's forces managed to establish headquarters in what was then a mostly undeveloped interior part of China. A flood of refugees, desperate to avoid Japanese control, trailed the Chinese troops inland. Historian James Bowen writes that the Nationalist military forces were "followed by hundreds of thousands of Chinese, of all classes and occupations, on foot, by cart, and by boat, and carrying what possessions they could save from the Japanese."[7]

Another War

By 1937 the already tense situation in Mongolia exploded into full-scale war. This conflict, the Second Sino-Japanese War, enabled Japan to conquer a large portion of Mongolia. It was an especially gruesome conflict that saw a number of horrifying atrocities, notably a massacre known as the Rape of Nanking. The Nanking carnage occurred when Japanese forces captured the city and over the course of six weeks looted it, raped thousands of women, and killed an estimated 250,000 to 300,000 Chinese—half of the city's population—including civilians and soldiers who had already surrendered. It was the worst single atrocity of the period encompassing the years before and during the world war. *New York Times* reporter Tillman Durdin described the scene of one incident:

> I drove down to the waterfront in my car. And to get to the gate I had to just climb over masses of bodies accumulated there. The

car just had to drive over these dead bodies. And the scene on the river front, as I waited for the launch . . . was of a group of smoking, chattering Japanese officers overseeing the massacring of a battalion of Chinese captured troops. They were marching about in groups of about 15, machine-gunning them.[8]

Back in Japan, the government tolerated no criticism of its actions from anyone, whether a government official or civilian. A journalist who was sympathetic to the government, Soho Tokutomi, summarized

Japanese soldiers prepare to bury Chinese captives alive, one of many atrocities committed during the massacre known as the Rape of Nanking. After capturing the city, Japanese forces raped thousands of women and killed hundreds of thousands of Chinese citizens, including many civilians.

this position when he noted, "The time has come for the Japanese to make up their minds to reject any who stand in the way of their country."[9] Political and military leaders did not hesitate to use violence in order to suppress dissent. Some military extremists were encouraged to intimidate and even assassinate politicians, businesspeople, and military leaders to further their goals.

One such instance involved a mutinous group of army officers, the so-called Young Officers. They assassinated several politicians who had dared to oppose the military. The Young Officers also unsuccessfully tried to kill several other politicians. In February 1936 the rebels surrounded the Japanese Foreign Office in Tokyo with troops and occupied much of the city for days. However, their plot to take over the government failed. In large part this was because the Japanese emperor, Hirohito (who had succeeded Emperor Meiji), took a strong stand against the Young Officers. The army high command chose to side with Hirohito and refused to support the insurgents.

The *Panay* Incident

Despite the suppression of dissent within Japan, it became clear to many observers that the military's dreams of expansion through violence were by no means held by all of the nation's people. Nowhere was this more evident than in the aftermath of the *Panay* Incident.

The *Panay* Incident was the first significant direct act of Japanese aggression against a Western power since the Russo-Japanese War. Late in 1937 Japanese aircraft attacked a convoy of American oil tankers, part of the US oil trade with China, that was making its way up China's Yangtze River. The convoy included the USS *Panay*, an American gunboat that was accompanying the tankers for protection. The Japanese sank the *Panay*, destroyed three of the oil tankers, and fired on survivors who were floating in the water. Three US soldiers and one Chinese soldier died in the incident. In addition, a number of American and Chinese sailors and civilians were wounded. The Japanese government formally apologized for this attack and paid the United States compensation, although it maintained that the attack had been a mistake.

This assault on American ships aroused an enormous wave of sympathy among the Japanese population. Many individuals visited the American embassy in Tokyo personally or mailed it letters and gifts of money. (Small amounts of money are traditional Japanese tokens of sympathy.) This compassionate response was a poignant demonstration that people in all walks of life, including doctors, professors, businesspeople, blue-collar workers, homemakers, and schoolchildren, wanted to apologize for the actions of the Japanese military. The US ambassador in Tokyo, Joseph Grew, commented in his memoirs, "That side of the [*Panay*] incident, at least, is profoundly touching and shows that at heart the Japanese are still a chivalrous people."[10]

Some civilians wrote directly to the US government in Washington, DC, to express their feelings. Among these was a group of thirty-seven Japanese schoolgirls in Tokyo. Their letter read:

> Dear Friend! This is a short letter, but we want to tell you how sorry we are for the mistake our airplane[s] made. We want you to forgive us I am little and do not understand very well, but I know they did not mean it. I feel so sorry for those who were hurt and killed.
>
> I am studying here at St. Margaret's school which was built by many American friends. I am studying English. But I am only thirteen and cannot write very well. All my school-mates are sorry like myself and wish you to forgive our country. To-morrow is X-mas, May it be merry, I hope the time will come when everybody can be friends. I wish you a Happy New Year. Good-bye.[11]

The Greater East Asia Co-Prosperity Sphere

Despite the wishes of these schoolgirls and countless other Japanese, relations between America and Japan continued to deteriorate in the wake of the *Panay* Incident. At the same time, a number of other nations were

The *Panay* Incident

When Japanese planes attacked American oil tankers on the Yangtze River in China in 1937, it was the first overt act of armed aggression by the Japanese against the United States. The Japanese government insisted that the attack on the convoy and the gunboat accompanying it, the USS *Panay*, had been a mistake. Historian Trevor K. Plante comments:

> Even after WWII, the exact motivation remained elusive. According to Commander Masatake Okumiya, who led the dive-bombers that Sunday in December it really was a case of mistaken identity. Japanese Army intelligence believed large numbers of Chinese troops were escaping from Nanking, and had specific information related to seven large merchant ships. They urged the Navy to attack these targets of opportunity. . . . By the time that case of mistaken identity had occurred, however, *Panay* was already at the bottom of the Yangtze.
>
> Others however, including many of the survivors, never believed the reason for the attacks could be so simple. If it really were a case of mistaken identity, why would the Japanese have seen fit to attack *Panay*—the only vessel in the convoy capable of firing back—first? And why would they continue to press the attack after flying low enough to identify the U.S. flags draped on the ship's awnings? How could they imagine that a simple merchant ship could fire back in its own defense, and with machine guns?

Trevor K. Plante, "Suddenly and Deliberately Attacked! The Story of the *Panay* Incident," USS *Panay* Memorial website. www.usspanay.org.

also closely monitoring the situation. The United Kingdom, France, and Netherlands were particularly concerned, since all three had significant colonial and territorial interests in eastern Asia.

These colonial powers, as well as the United States, were already supplying economic assistance to China's Nationalist forces. Now, following the *Panay* Incident, they stepped this up by applying economic pressure on Japan. Notably, they imposed severe embargoes during this period—that is, they banned the export of goods to that country. The United States, which had once been one of Japan's major trading partners, also froze Japanese assets in America.

These economic obstacles somewhat slowed Japan's aggression, but the nation was still far from powerless, and it continued to expand its control over the region. Using the slogan "Asia for Asians," pro-expansion Japanese leaders emphasized their desire to free Asia of Western colonial influence—by force if necessary. This goal took on a new dimension in the summer of 1940 when Japan announced the creation of an entity it called the Greater East Asia Co-Prosperity Sphere (also known as the New Order). According to the Japanese government, creating this organization was the only way for the nation to survive. The Japanese premier, Prince Fumimaro Konoe, asserted that the Co-Prosperity Sphere was "absolutely necessary to the continued existence of this country."[12]

The Co-Prosperity Sphere was designed to be a unified group of nations that would be self-sufficient and completely free of Western authority. Among the regions singled out as potential partners in the Sphere were Burma, the Philippines, a portion of India, and the regions that today are Thailand, Vietnam, Laos, and Cambodia, as well as several small Pacific islands.

Japan's leaders adamantly stated that they were willing to bring these regions into the group only through peaceful negotiations. However, Japan's military occupation of Manchuria and Mongolia had plainly demonstrated its readiness to use force if needed. Bowen comments, "The Japanese made it quite clear that any country resisting inclusion in their Greater East Asia Co-Prosperity Sphere would be treated as an enemy of Japan."[13]

A New Form of Colonization

Japan was not able to fulfill its dream of comprehensively bringing all of eastern Asia into the Co-Prosperity Sphere. However, it did succeed in annexing several regions in addition to the portions of China it already occupied. These new territories included Formosa (today Taiwan), Korea, a number of South Pacific islands, and part of the Russian Far East.

According to the official Japanese line, membership in the Co-Prosperity Sphere would be good for all of its member countries, since each would be able to maintain its own separate economic, political, and social structures. But the plan was clearly tilted to Japan's advantage. For one thing, the scheme was designed to give Japan—and only Japan—control over a number of militarily strategic points across eastern Asia. The lopsided economic advantage in favor of Japan was also clear, and the need for this was especially sharp because its expansionist plans were creating an enormous drain on its economic and human resources. Historian Gordon W. Prange comments, "Though [Japan] tried desperately to 'solve' what it euphemistically termed the China incident [and later invasions], it remained in a whirlpool that sucked down thousands upon thousands of its young men, tons upon tons of military equipment, and millions of yen."[14]

And so it quickly became clear that the Co-Prosperity Sphere was mutually beneficial in name only. Put simply, it did nothing more than replace the previously existing Western colonial powers with another colonial power. As in Manchuria, Japan's "cooperation" with other countries involved essentially creating a series of puppet governments that remained under Tokyo's control. History professor Bill Gordon writes, "The Co-Prosperity Sphere turned out to be just another form of oppressive imperialism in place of the imperialism previously imposed by Western nations."[15]

The Reality of Co-Prosperity

As has happened in colonial relationships throughout history, the reality of "co-prosperity" in eastern Asia meant that the people of the occupied countries were often subject to harsh conditions and cruel treatment. For one thing, Japanese officials overseeing the colonies typically suppressed local customs, languages, and beliefs, forcing citizens to accept instead a program of Japanization. Far worse than these policies of suppression were widespread instances of forced labor, as well as incidents involving the torture and execution of dissidents.

Japan's triumph in the Russo-Japanese War had emboldened its military leaders to turn their country's dreams of territorial expansion into reality, and by the late 1930s they had brought significant portions of eastern Asia under their control. But Japan's aggressive policies and outright acts of war also brought its relations with Western countries nearly to the breaking point. This was especially true in the case of the United States, whose control of the Philippines and the Hawaiian Islands was considered by Japan to be a serious obstacle. American authorities, in turn, asserted that ongoing Japanese incursions posed clear threats to American interests and to overall stability and peace in the region. And so both sides began planning for the possibility that they might go to war.

Chapter 2

The Buildup to War

Japan's creation of the Co-Prosperity Sphere had hinged on its vow to free eastern Asian nations from their status as colonies. Key to this declaration was a rejection of Western influence—that is, putting the slogan "Asia for Asians" into practice. However, Japan's leaders were at this point concerned only with controlling eastern Asia. They saw no problem in allying themselves with Western nations that were fighting to invade and occupy other parts of the globe.

And so events took a dramatic turn in the fall of 1940. Japan aligned itself with the Axis powers, Germany and Italy, with an agreement called the Tripartite Pact. A key part of this alliance was the promise the three countries made to come to each other's aid if a neutral country—in particular, the United States—made the first move in an armed conflict. Another important element was an agreement to cooperate in administering occupied territories. So, when France and Netherlands fell to Nazi Germany in 1940, Japan established military bases in the Dutch East Indies and French Indochina. Japan's empire also grew to include German commercial interests in China and several Pacific island chains previously held by Germany.

Planning for a Short, Quick Attack

Despite this growth in its empire, Japan's long-range plans for a Pacific war were, in a sense, limited. Specifically, many of its top military leaders did not believe that it could sustain a war against the Allies, especially the United States, for more than about a year. So in 1940 they began in earnest planning for a brief, concentrated attack on several spots across the Pacific. The strategy was to attack without waging an extended war, then force a peace settlement to Japan's advantage.

Although the Japanese targeted several ports around the Pacific, the chief focus of this strategy was Pearl Harbor. The Japanese military knew that crippling the American fleet stationed there would severely limit the ability of the United States to fight in the Pacific. It would also isolate bases in the secondary American target, the Philippines, by cutting off the main supply routes between that region and the US mainland.

Not all Japanese military officers agreed with this strategy, however. The most important of these dissidents was Isoroku Yamamoto, the commander in chief of the Imperial Navy. Yamamoto was convinced that an attack would cause the United States to fiercely retaliate and crush Japan. Although personally committed to Japan's expansionist policies, he argued that Japan could not win an extended war and thus settling the issue through diplomacy was the only reasonable option. However, Yamamoto was overruled and, ironically, assigned to be the chief architect of the Pearl Harbor operation. Although he remained skeptical, Yamamoto had no choice but to carry out his orders. Gordon W. Prange comments on this irony: "Probably no man in Japan more earnestly wanted to avoid war with the United States than the one who planned the Pearl Harbor attack."[16]

Setting Sail for Hawaii

Through the summer and fall of 1941, Yamamoto oversaw preparations for an attack. Japan's military forces trained air and naval personnel, stockpiled supplies, and readied ships and airplanes. Care was taken to tailor the attack plans to the specifics of the target. For example, pilots trained using a harbor on the southern island of Kyushu that resembled Pearl Harbor's shallow waters, and special bombs were designed to have maximum effectiveness in such a situation.

Like Yamamoto, Emperor Hirohito had deep personal misgivings about the attack plans. He strongly felt that diplomatic talks should

Pearl Harbor (pictured) was the primary target of the Japanese military in planning for its initial attacks in the Pacific. The idea was to cripple the US fleet and thus severely limit its fighting ability.

take precedence over war preparations, and debate on this point continued in Tokyo throughout the summer. Nonetheless, Japan's military leaders convinced Hirohito of the importance of preparing for an attack, insisting that they would launch it only if diplomacy failed. Hirohito agreed to this compromise—and negotiations began almost immediately.

Japan's preparations for war were completed in the late fall of 1941, and on November 26 a Japanese convoy consisting of six aircraft carriers with a total of 408 aircraft accompanied by fuel tankers and other supporting ships sailed toward Hawaii from northern Japan. This fleet was, at the time, the most powerful single carrier force and the greatest concentration of air power in the history of naval warfare. Overall, Japan now had the third-largest navy in the world, surpassed only by Great Britain and the United States. This size and power was crucial, since Japan needed a strong presence at sea to protect its coastlines and transport supplies. H.P. Willmott notes, "The story of the Japanese attack on the US . . . is the story of sea power and naval powers."[17]

America Prepares

As Japan made its preparations for a possible war, the United States did the same. Serious discussions about US involvement in conflict in the Pacific, in Europe, or both had been taking place since the 1930s. American authorities were generally more concerned with the Pacific, since Japan was more likely to directly invade from the west than were Germany and Italy from across the Atlantic. For this reason, the United States had steadily increased its military presence in the Pacific. This included building or strengthening existing bases on remote Pacific islands, in Hawaii, in the Philippines, and along the West Coast of the mainland.

A major part of these plans was a decision by president Franklin D. Roosevelt in 1940 to move the bulk of his Pacific Fleet to Pearl Harbor from its base in San Diego, California. Roosevelt's reasoning was that placing this fleet's formidable power closer to Japanese-controlled territory would discourage the Japanese from launching an attack.

The president's decision was a highly controversial one at the time. The most vocal critic was Admiral James O. Richardson, commander in chief of the Pacific Fleet, who felt strongly that stationing his forces at Pearl Harbor, so close to possible attack, was a serious miscalculation. He proved to be right, and in the ensuing decades some historians have suggested that moving the fleet was the greatest single mistake the United States made in the war.

Expectations

Another controversial decision—in retrospect, clearly a crucial error—was to allow Pearl Harbor to be insufficiently ready for an attack. There were several reasons for this. Notably, most American strategists believed that the Philippines, not Hawaii, would be the Japanese military's main target, since US forces there posed a serious threat to Japan's ability to transport supplies by sea. There was also widespread belief that any secondary targets would be in British and Dutch holdings—not American territories.

At the same time, American authorities believed that Japan would not be able to mount major attacks on multiple fronts across the vast stretches of water from Southeast Asia to Hawaii. Willmott comments, "It seemed frankly inconceivable that the Japanese would instigate a move against a base which was 4,000 miles from their home islands, and still less to do so in conjunction with a number of offensives staged across the 6,000 miles of ocean from Hawaii to south-east Asia."[18]

Furthermore, Pearl Harbor was already considered unusually secure by most of the top US authorities. This was reflected in a letter General George C. Marshall, the US Army chief of staff, sent to Roosevelt in April 1941. Marshall asserted, "The defense of Oahu, due to its fortification, its garrison, and its physical characteristics, is believed to be the strongest fortress in the world."[19]

Because of this confidence, a number of defensive precautions were allowed to slip. For example, long-range air patrols around the Hawaiian Islands were not made often or very far out to sea, so there could have been little warning of an approaching fleet. Also, it was not considered a priority to have B-17 bombers, among the most important parts of the army air corps arsenal, in Hawaii. (The army air corps was the predecessor of the air force of today.) US military strategists instead concentrated their bombers in the Philippines.

Overall, then, to most American observers Hawaii seemed like an unlikely target. At the same time, indications that Pearl Harbor was, in fact, not as secure as thought were widely ignored. For example, when defensive drills were conducted, the results indicated that its forces would not be able to stop an air attack. But these results were not taken seriously. During one such drill, the defensive team expected a traditional assault from the sea, and the team was caught by surprise when a wave of offensive planes, hidden by rain clouds, suddenly swooped down. Writer John Toland comments, "It should have been a cautionary lesson but the Chief Umpire [of the drill] concluded: 'It is doubtful if air attacks can be launched against Oahu in the face of strong defensive

B-17 Flying Fortresses make deadly bombing runs over Nazi-held territory in Austria in 1944. Before the Pearl Harbor attack, America's B-17 fleet was concentrated in the Philippines, which was considered at greater risk of Japanese attack than Hawaii.

aviation without . . . great losses to the attacking air force.' The Japanese took a different view."[20]

In retrospect the Japanese perspective proved correct. Looking back in 1948 on the situation, General Sherman Miles, chief of the US Army Military Intelligence Division when Pearl Harbor was attacked, commented, "Wherever or whenever Washington may have thought the Japanese cat would probably jump, Hawaii's primary mission was to meet it there if it came. Yet both the Army and Navy commands there acted as if there were no chance of a Japanese overseas attack on them. What they actually did and did not do simply spelled 'It can't happen here.'"[21]

Spies in Hawaii

In the period just prior to the Pearl Harbor attack, Japan carried out a variety of intelligence operations, including having several spies in Hawaii. Major General Charles D. Herron, the head of the US Army's Hawaiian Command, commented, "It was a matter of common knowledge that the Japanese consulate in Honolulu was the hotbed of espionage in Oahu."

One of these spies was a young Imperial Navy officer, Ensign Takeo Yoshikawa. Yoshikawa was assigned to the Japanese embassy in Honolulu, using the name Tadashi Morimura. The spy collected intelligence in several ways, including visiting Pearl Harbor seemingly just to sketch it, taking a tour boat ride, and gossiping with taxi drivers. Among the vital intelligence he found was detailed information on what ships were in the harbor (although he failed to note that America's three aircraft carriers were not in port). He also advised that attacking on a Sunday would be best, because that was the day when the largest number of sailors would be on shore leave and away from the harbor.

Quoted in Gordon W. Prange, *At Dawn We Slept*. New York: Penguin, 1982, p. 70.

Other Problems

The US military was ill prepared for a surprise attack in other ways besides letting Pearl Harbor's defenses slip. Notably, its ability to gather and analyze military intelligence, while extensive, was not especially effective. For one thing, it proved difficult to break the Japanese military's complex coded messages. An article written for the US Army Center of Military History points out, "During the first part of the war, the performance of the Army's signal intelligence organization was somewhat disappointing. . . . It found its main task—coping with the mysteries of Japanese military communications—intractable."[22]

Furthermore, the main agencies responsible for intercepting, translating, decoding, and forwarding Japanese messages—the army's Signal Intelligence Service (SIS) and the navy's Office of Naval Intelligence (ONI)—were severely overworked and understaffed. For example, at the time of the attack on Pearl Harbor, the SIS had a staff of only 331, divided among its Washington, DC, headquarters and a string of field offices. Adding to these problems was the fact that the SIS and ONI had a long-standing rivalry and often refused to cooperate with each other. In part because of this hobbled intelligence-gathering ability, America intercepted many Japanese messages indicating the possibility of an attack—but none that specifically mentioned Pearl Harbor. The United States continued to assume that the Philippines would be the primary target.

As America prepared its contingency plans, the issue of timing became crucial. Roosevelt and his advisers agreed that they could not make the first move in any conflict. If they did, according to the Tripartite Act, Germany and Italy could legitimately provide aid to Japan. This was made clear on November 27, 1941, when Marshall sent a message to all commands in the Pacific. He made it clear that American forces were to continue defensive precautions and attack only in a dire emergency:

> Japanese future action unpredictable but hostile action possible at any moment. If hostilities cannot, repeat cannot, be avoided the United States desires that Japan commit the first overt act. This policy should not, repeat not, be construed as restricting you to a course of action that might jeopardize your defense. Prior to hostile Japanese action you are directed to undertake such reconnaissance and other measures as you deem necessary.[23]

Diplomatic Talks Go Nowhere

As military preparations on both sides continued, intense diplomatic talks were also taking place. Their purpose was to find a compromise that would satisfy both Japan and the Allies. As Hirohito had instructed, any decision to launch an attack hinged on the outcome of these talks. If they proved inconclusive, the Japanese convoy at sea was to launch an assault on Pearl Harbor. Tokyo ordered its ships to get into position and await word before proceeding.

The diplomatic talks began in 1941 in Washington, DC, between Japanese ambassador Kichisaburo Nomura and US secretary of state Cordell Hull. Their discussions remained cordial on the surface, typified by such diplomatic words as this statement from the Japanese embassy: "The United States does not understand the real situation in East Asia. It is . . . tending to obstruct the construction of the New Order. This is extremely regrettable."[24]

But the diplomats' polite language masked an increasingly tense and hostile situation. Underlying the talks was a realization that the growing animosity between Japan and the United States was about to explode. Neither side was willing to significantly change its position.

Nomura insisted that his country needed to retain most of its occupied lands. He argued that this centralized authority was the only way to stabilize the region. Nomura also demanded an end to American military maneuvers in the Pacific. The Japanese ambassador asserted that such an agreement, or an acceptable variation, was necessary "to prevent from getting beyond control the Japanese public opinion which had been dangerously aroused because of the successive measures taken by the United States, Great Britain and Netherlands East Indies against Japan."[25]

No Compromise

Hull, for his part, insisted that Japan make deep compromises. He wanted a guarantee that Japan would withdraw from Indochina and much of the territory it occupied in China. He also demanded that Japan dissolve the Co-Prosperity Sphere and weaken its ties to Germany and Italy. Hull summed his position up when he asked Nomura how the Japanese government could expect the United States "to sit absolutely quiet while two or three nations [the Axis powers] before our very eyes organized naval and military forces and went out and conquered the balance of the earth, including the seven seas and all trade routes and the other four continents."[26]

A number of compromises were suggested, such as Hull's suggestion that Indochina become a neutral territory. Another proposal, made by Nomura, would have guaranteed, among other things, that Japan would not expand into areas adjoining Indochina, and that it would not take military action in a region south of Japan "without any justifiable reason."[27] In return the United States would agree to stop sending supplies to the Nationalist forces in China.

However, each side forcefully rejected the compromise solutions proposed by the other. When it became clear that Nomura and Hull were getting nowhere, Japan sent Saburo Kurusu, another high-level diplomat, to Washington to assist. However, Kurusu brought no new plans or proposals to the talks, and US authorities remained skeptical of Japan's sincerity. Diplomacy was at a standstill.

On December 6, 1941, Roosevelt tried to break this diplomatic logjam by sending a telegram directly to Hirohito. In contrast to the pragmatic talks that had taken place, this was a highly personal message, indicating sadness that the impasse was robbing both sides of compassion. Roosevelt further stated that only tragedy would ensue if the problem could not be resolved, adding that both he and the emperor had "a sacred duty to restore traditional amity [goodwill] and prevent further death and destruction in the world."[28]

No More Talk

There is no evidence that Hirohito ever received Roosevelt's message. Either way, nothing changed; further discussion seemed pointless. The talks formally ended on December 7, 1941. The catalyst was a five-thousand-word document from Tokyo to the Japanese embassy in Washington, DC. This memorandum is usually called the Fourteen-Point Message or the Final Message. In it Tokyo instructed Kurusu and Nomura to formally break off the talks. This was to take place at exactly

The Fourteen-Point Message

Delivery of a final memorandum, the so-called Fourteen-Point Message, from the Japanese government on December 7, 1941, was a crucial turning point. It instructed Japanese diplomats to break off diplomatic talks with the United States. This end of peaceful negotiations was Japan's declaration of war, even though it was delivered after the attack on Pearl Harbor had begun. Below is an excerpt from this historic message.

> From the beginning . . . the Japanese Government has always maintained an attitude of fairness and moderation, and did its best to reach a settlement. . . .
>
> It is a fact of history that the countries of East Asia have for the past two hundred years or more been compelled to observe the status quo under the Anglo-American policy of imperialistic exploitation. . . . The Japanese Government cannot tolerate the perpetuation of such a situation. . . .
>
> Obviously it is the intention of the American Government to conspire with Great Britain and other countries to obstruct Japan's effort toward the establishment of peace through the creation of a new order in East Asia. . . . This intention has been revealed clearly during the course of the present negotiation. . . .
>
> Thus the earnest hope of the Japanese Government to adjust Japanese-American relations and to preserve and promote the peace of the Pacific through cooperation with the American Government has finally been lost.
>
> The Japanese Government regrets to have to notify hereby the American Government that in view of the attitude of the American Government it cannot but consider that it is impossible to reach an agreement through further negotiations.

Quoted in HyperWar, "Japanese 'Fourteen Part' Message of December 7, 1941." www.ibiblio.org.

1:00 p.m. eastern time on December 7. (Because of the international date line, it was December 8 in Tokyo.) The timing proved to be a crucial point.

Nomura and Kurusu requested an appointment with Hull for that hour. However, they did not deliver the message at the appointed time. In part this was because Tokyo had not emphasized the importance of the exact timing. But there was another reason: The Japanese embassy's work to decrypt, translate into English, and type the message into a final, corrected copy was complex and time-consuming. Compounding the delay was the fact that the person responsible for writing up this final copy, First Secretary Katsuzo Okumura, was a poor typist.

As a result, Nomura and Kurusu rescheduled their appointment with Hull for 1:45 p.m. But the Japanese delegation did not arrive at Hull's office until 2:05, and the two sides did not meet until 2:20. The message the Japanese delivered asserted that the United States was solely responsible for blocking peace talks. It stated that the United States had "resorted to every possible measure to assist the Chungking [Chinese resistance] regime so as to obstruct the establishment of a general peace between Japan and China"[29] and that America had "attempted to frustrate Japan's aspiration to the ideal of common prosperity in cooperation with these regions."[30]

The Next Step: War

The message went on to reiterate Japan's position that the United States was being intolerably aggressive by preparing for the strong possibility of entering the European war and by continuing its military buildup in the Pacific. In conclusion Tokyo noted that "in view of the attitude of the American Government [Japan] cannot but consider that it is impossible to reach an agreement through further negotiations."[31]

The careful wording of the Fourteen-Point Message clearly broke off diplomatic negotiations, but it stopped short of an outright declaration of war. Nonetheless, Hull interpreted the notice as such, and his response was quick and furious. He told Nomura and Kurusu:

> I must say that in all my conversations with you . . . during the last nine months I have never uttered one word of untruth. This is borne out absolutely by the record. In all my fifty years of public service I have never seen a document that was more crowded with infamous falsehoods and distortions—infamous falsehoods and distortions on a scale so huge that I never imagined until today that any Government on this planet was capable of uttering them.[32]

By this time, it seemed, there was no turning back. The decades of animosity between Japan and the West, particularly the United States, had culminated in the complete collapse of talks designed to stave off war. Both sides had already made extensive military preparations in case the talks ended badly. Now a new chapter in history was about to begin.

Chapter 3

The Attack

As the diplomats in Washington sparred, the impending attack on Pearl Harbor was shaping up thousands of miles and six time zones away. By dawn on December 7, 1941, the naval task force that had sailed from Japan was stationed some 250 miles (402km) off the coast of Oahu, awaiting word of the final meeting in Washington, DC. That meeting's scheduled hour, because of the time difference, was 7:00 a.m. in Hawaii. Waiting for the message was a nerve-racking time for the Japanese fleet. Rear Admiral Sadatoshi Tomioka later recalled that the voyage to Hawaii and the tense waiting at sea was "the most difficult and agonizing period for every officer in the Naval General Staff who knew about Pearl Harbor."[33]

Depending on the message, the fleet would either return home or attack thirty minutes after the scheduled time—that is, 7:30 a.m. Hawaii time. If this had happened on schedule, the assault would have started just after the formal end of negotiations, in accordance with internationally agreed conventions. But Tokyo broke those rules by sending the fleet a coded message: "Climb Mt. Niitaka"[34]—the signal for the attack to start—at the exact moment of the scheduled meeting. Tomioka and his fellow officers were unaware that the message to Hull had been delayed. As a result, Japan launched its attack nearly two hours early.

For decades, historians blamed this on the Japanese embassy's failure to deliver the message on time. However, documents discovered in 1999 proved otherwise. Takeo Iguchi, a professor at International Christian University in Tokyo, while doing research in Japan's Imperial War Library, discovered a secret war diary—that is, a record kept by Japan's military leaders—indicating that Tokyo had planned all along to attack early. It noted approvingly on the day before the attack, "Our deceptive diplomacy is steadily proceeding toward success."[35] Iguchi comments, "The diary shows that the army and navy did not want to give any proper declaration of war, or indeed prior notice even of the termination of negotiations."[36]

Tokyo apparently deliberately caused the delay by including in the message several phrases that were obscure, garbled, difficult to translate, or ambiguous. As far as Iguchi can determine, the diplomats in Washington were not aware of this deception. Whether or not this was true, *New York Times* reporter Howard W. French notes, "The picture that emerges from the papers is one of a breathtakingly cunning deceit by Tokyo aimed at avoiding any hint to the Roosevelt administration of Japan's hostile intentions."[37]

Delivering the Message

As events were unfolding in Washington, DC, the US military intercepted and analyzed the Fourteen-Point Message on its own. However, its delivery to Marshall, the army's chief of staff, was delayed. Time was lost decoding and translating the message, and even then the general was not immediately informed. He was unavailable because he was taking his usual Sunday morning horseback ride. Marshall later testified before a congressional committee that he acted as soon as he returned. The general called the president and ordered a message sent to every American base in the Pacific, ordering them to go on high alert. He told the committee, "I hung up the White House telephone and wrote out a message in longhand."[38]

There were further delays. The army's unreliable radio communication system failed. The navy offered the use of its separate communications link, but the two rivals were still hostile toward each other. Army radio officers, not realizing the importance of Marshall's message, declined. According to the official site of the organization that operates today's tours of Pearl Harbor, "There was a complete lack of cooperation between the Army and Navy."[39]

Attempts were made to send the message along the RCA network's commercial facilities, but this was not immediately successful, and the

Eyewitness to History

Thousands of military personnel died at Pearl Harbor, but thousands more survived. *Washington Post* reporter Sylvia Carignan recounts the story of one survivor:

> Around 8 a.m. on Dec. 7, 1941, Army Private Francis Stueve sat down to breakfast with the rest of the 89th Field Artillery battalion, stationed at Pearl Harbor.
>
> "As quiet a day as you've ever seen," Stueve remembers now. "Beautiful sunshine, nothing going on." Suddenly, not far from his seat in the dining hall: bang, bang, bang.
>
> "Somebody says, 'It's the Chinese New Year,'" he said. But then, a bullet broke through the glass window of the dining hall. Another flew just past Stueve and knocked the butter dish off the table. . . . Bewildered by the bullet, Stueve, then 24, and a few other men ran outside.
>
> "We're looking at the clouds, and watched a Japanese plane that had its signals on," he said.
>
> It was common for American planes to practice maneuvers, Stueve said, but he soon realized the Japanese plane was bent on attacking his base and his fellow soldiers.
>
> "We were getting shot like everything was going to be destroyed," he said. Soldiers fell left and right, buildings were hit by gunfire and ships suffered fatal gashes.
>
> "We had so many casualties. It's a hard thing to do when people are screaming for aid . . . and you don't have nobody coming," he said. "Some who were looking out for their own were also getting killed."

Sylvia Carignan, "Pearl Harbor Attacked: A Witness Remembers, 70 Years Later," *Washington Post,* December 6, 2011. www.washingtonpost.com.

message was even further delayed. When it finally arrived at RCA's facilities in Hawaii, a motorcycle messenger left to deliver the news to the authorities at Pearl Harbor. But a few minutes after he rode away, the attack began, and he was caught in the chaos. The messenger managed to deliver his warning—hours after the attack had ended. Many historians feel that the delays did not matter. Even if the message had been received immediately, Pearl would not have had time to prepare. Sherman Miles comments, "There would not have been sufficient time to bridge the gap, mental and material, between the status of the Hawaiian commands on that quiet Sunday morning and one of effective alert."[40]

"Don't Worry About It"

The morning of December 7, 1941, was indeed unremarkable. Most of Pearl Harbor's sailors and soldiers were away from their stations, on shore leave, at church, or otherwise off duty. However, there was one incident of hostile action. At 3:42 a.m., the periscope of a midget Japanese submarine was spotted near the entrance to the harbor. The destroyer USS *Ward* responded and sank it at 6:37 a.m. Shortly afterward, at 7:02 a.m., two young army radio operators, Privates George Elliott Jr. and Joseph Lockard, spotted something approaching by air from the north—the opposite end of Oahu from Pearl Harbor. In 1941 radar was a new and unfamiliar technology, and the radar stations on Oahu were being used only for training purposes. Elliott and Lockard were practicing with it when they detected aircraft approaching. The aircraft were about 130 miles (209km) out—near the limit of the radar's reach. Elliott and Lockard telephoned Lieutenant Kermit A. Tyler, who was in charge of the aircraft tracking center at Fort Shafter near Honolulu.

But Tyler, who was also young and untrained and had been at Shafter for only two days, did not realize the significance of the sighting. There were several reasons for this. Tyler assumed that the planes were American B-17 bombers expected from the mainland along that course and around that time. Also, the radar operators did not realize that there were more than fifty planes in the convoy—far more than expected. Furthermore, Elliott and Lockard were as inexperienced as Tyler. Tyler later recalled, "I knew the [radar] equipment was pretty new. In fact, the guy who was on the scope, who first detected the planes, it was the first time he'd ever sat at the scope. So I figured they were pretty green and had not had any opportunity to view a flight of B-17s coming in. Common sense said, Well, these are the B-17s. So I told them, 'Don't worry about it.'"[41]

Elliott and Lockard continued to monitor the incoming planes for practice. As the fleet grew near, they saw that it appeared much larger than the expected American convoy. However, they assumed that their equipment was faulty. When the airplanes disappeared behind a

Japanese dive bombers warm up on the deck of an aircraft carrier in the Pacific shortly before launching the attack on Pearl Harbor. US military personnel initially mistook the Japanese planes heading their way for American B-17s coming from the mainland.

mountain range at 7:45 a.m., Elliott and Lockard turned their equipment off. They left the base to get breakfast and did not realize what was happening until it was too late.

Tyler, Elliott, and Lockard were never held responsible for their errors, and there was little that could have been done even if they had immediately issued an alert. It seemed like a small decision at the time, but Tyler's response to the report—"Don't worry about it"—had enormous repercussions. After Tyler's death in 2010, *New York Times* reporter Richard Goldstein commented, "They were only four words, but they made him a footnote figure in a catastrophic day for America and shadowed him the rest of his long life."[42]

The Attack Begins

It took about two hours for the first wave of Japanese airplanes, led by Captain Mitsuo Fuchida, to fly from their position at sea to Oahu. Only a few minutes after Elliot and Lockard turned off their equipment, the attack force had crossed the island from north to south and at 7:48 a.m. arrived at Pearl Harbor.

Several US planes were in the air over the island on routine patrol at the time. When one of the American planes spotted the incoming convoy, it frantically sent a message to base. But the message was garbled and could not be understood. At the same time, ships just outside the mouth of the harbor also spotted the Japanese planes and issued warnings.

As with the radar operators, however, it is unlikely that these messages could have significantly changed events, because the Japanese planes immediately started bombing and strafing American facilities. Fuchida, the Japanese flight commander, radioed to his shipboard headquarters a now-famous phrase: "*Tora! Tora! Tora!*"[43] (Tiger! Tiger! Tiger!). This code phrase indicated that the attack had begun.

At about 7:50 a.m., just as the attack began, the navy yard signal tower sent a frantic signal to the rest of the base: "ENEMY AIR RAID—NOT DRILL."[44] A second wave followed the first almost immediately. Rear admiral Husband Kimmel, commander in chief of the US Pacific

Fleet, later noted in a memo to the secretary of the navy, "From then on there was almost continuous enemy air activity of some kind over the harbor, but there seemed to be separate periods of intense activity as if different new waves were arriving prior to departure of last one."[45]

The primary targets were the large ships moored along "Battleship Row," on the east side of Ford Island in the harbor. However, the incoming attackers also focused on other facilities in the area, including the army air corps's Hickam, Bellows, and Wheeler Fields. Writing in the *New York Times* the next day, reporter Frank L. Kluckhorn described the scene: "Japanese bombers, with the red circle of the Rising Sun of Japan on their wings, suddenly appeared, [escorted] by fighters. Flying high, they suddenly dive-bombed, attacking Pearl Harbor, the great Navy base, the [adjoining] Army's Hickam Field and Ford Island."[46]

Unprepared

Japanese military leaders had carefully chosen the timing of the attack so that the Americans had only skeleton crews on duty. This minimized the number of casualties, but that was not the point: The Japanese knew that skeleton crews would be less effective at returning fire.

The Japanese were at a further advantage because the United States did not consider the base a primary target, so Pearl Harbor was not on high alert and extra precautions had not been taken. For example, there were no antisubmarine nets at the mouth of the harbor. The army air corps fleet was on the ground, in the open and not hidden inside hangars. Also, the planes were wingtip to wingtip, preventing quick departures. As a result, only eight pilots managed to get airborne during the attack itself. Furthermore, the base's antiaircraft guns were unmanned, and ammunition storage units were locked in accordance with peacetime regulations.

In the harbor the situation was equally dire. In some cases sailors were able to return fire or maneuver away. For example, although a bomb tore a hole in the battleship USS *Nevada*'s side, the ship was able to get away from Battleship Row because it was not tied up alongside the other vessels. As the crew of the *Nevada* frantically fired on Japanese planes,

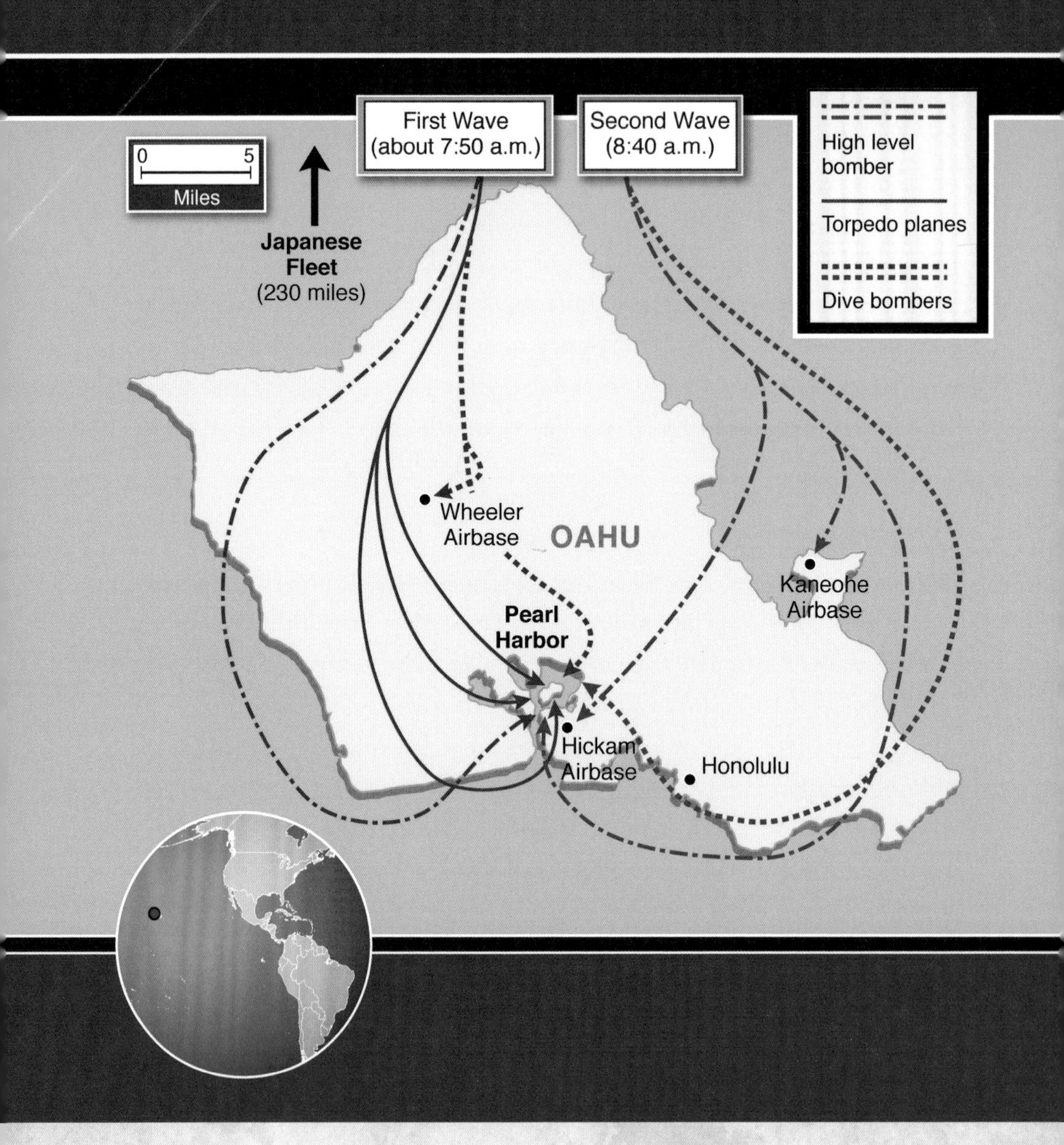

its officers tried to sail to the main navy yard on the mainland. At least five Japanese planes were brought down by gunfire from the *Nevada*, but the ship was too badly damaged to continue. Its officers decided to deliberately beach the vessel to keep it from blocking the harbor.

Other ships, still tied to their docks, suffered even more devastating damage. One of these was the battleship USS *Utah*, which had only one senior officer aboard when it was hit. Three planes suddenly appeared overhead just as crew members were raising the morning flag, and moments later the planes dropped their payloads of bombs. Within minutes, the *Utah* was sinking and its crew was ordered to abandon ship. Some of the sailors who jumped into the water were rescued by small boats from the *Utah*, while others swam ashore, avoiding strafing as best they could. Some did not make it to safety.

The most serious single blow was to the USS *Arizona*. Ten bombers homed in on the ship and scored four direct hits. One powerful bomb crashed through the ship's armored decks and ignited a magazine (a storage area for explosives). The resulting blast ripped the ship's sides open in seconds, and fire engulfed it. Within minutes, the *Arizona* had sunk, and 1,177 of its crew members were dead or dying—including twenty-three sets of brothers and one father and son. This single disaster represented nearly half of the entire loss of American life during the attack.

The Attack Ends

The attack lasted about two hours and ended as abruptly as it began. Historian C. Peter Chen, using military terminology to denote time, notes, "By 0940, most Japanese aircraft had left the vicinity, but American anti-aircraft fire continued to fire at any sign of hostile movement [and by] 1000, the skies over Pearl Harbor were clear."[47] John Finn, a navy airman, adds a chilling personal recollection: "After the last plane passed over, there was absolute silence, other than planes crackling and burning."[48]

As Pearl Harbor smoldered and survivors of the attack struggled with the chaos, the Japanese planes returned to their carriers. The mission's leaders considered sending a third wave to destroy virtually all of the remaining naval fleet, but they decided against it for several reasons. One was that it would have taken several hours for a third wave to reach the target, by which time the remaining American planes would be ready to fight back. Another reason was that the Japanese carriers were running low on the fuel needed to replenish the airplanes.

So the Japanese commanders decided that their primary mission—crippling the US naval fleet—was enough. As soon as its surviving planes had returned, the task force set sail for home. American ships and planes tried to catch up, but they were too slow, and the Japanese ships crossed the ocean unscathed.

The Losses

Once the attack was over, the long process of recovery began for the Americans. The survivors attended to the wounded, recovered the bodies of the dead, assessed the damage to facilities and vessels, began the repair process, and decided what came next.

The deaths, both military and civilian, naturally constituted the greatest loss. The casualties were stunning: On the American side, 2,335 military personnel were killed, missing, or died later of wounds, and 1,143 were wounded but survived. Among American civilians, 68 were killed, missing, or died later of wounds, and 33 were wounded but survived.

The material losses were also enormous. Of the more than 90 military ships at anchor, a total of 21 were destroyed. Eight battleships, which were among the most important components of the naval fleet, were sunk or badly damaged. Three light cruisers, 3 destroyers, and 3 smaller vessels were among the other destroyed ships. At the same time, 188 aircraft (out of 402) were destroyed, and another 159 were damaged. The vast majority of these were hit before they had a chance to take off.

On the other hand, a significant portion of Pearl Harbor's facilities, including its fuel tanks and power station, sustained minimal or no damage, since they had not been primary targets. More importantly, the Pacific Fleet's three aircraft carriers, the most valuable ships of all, had escaped destruction. The Japanese had been given faulty information, and these ships—the *Lexington*, the *Enterprise*, and the *Saratoga*—were hundreds of miles away. The *Enterprise* and the *Lexington* were deliver-

The USS Arizona *sinks within minutes of a powerful blast that ripped open the ship's sides and engulfed it in fire. The loss of life on this one ship represented nearly half of the American deaths from the attack.*

ing fighter planes to bases on remote Wake and Midway Islands, and the *Saratoga* was being refitted at the naval shipyards in Bremerton, Washington.

Compared with these American losses, Japan's casualties were light. Only twenty-nine planes—less than 10 percent of the attacking force—did not return to their carriers. The five midget submarines that had tried to penetrate the inner harbor were also lost. Altogether, sixty-four Japanese military personnel were killed, and one was captured when his sub was forced to beach itself on the eastern shore of Oahu. This sailor, Kazuo Sakamaki, became the first prisoner of war in the Pacific conflict.

No Excuse

Almost immediately after the attack on Pearl Harbor, critics began to condemn the US military for not being well enough prepared for it. In this passage, writer Gordon W. Prange sums up these criticisms:

> No attitude on the part of Washington, no lack of equipment or funds can explain or excuse the failure to establish at least approach lines or a reporting system to account for planes in Hawaiian skies. All that such procedures required was an appreciation of the value of incoming aircraft identification and fighter direction—abundantly displayed in the Battle of Britain [earlier in the war]—plus a little initiative and cooperation. But unfortunately those qualities . . . appear to have been missing.

Gordon W. Prange, *At Dawn We Slept*. New York: Penguin, 1982, p. 730.

Salvaging the Wrecks

For several months following the raid, Pearl Harbor personnel completed a staggering amount of salvage work. Among the tasks carried out were the roughly twenty thousand hours that navy and civilian divers spent underwater. This work was done to raise the damaged ships where possible, recover human remains, and salvage documents, ammunition, and other items that lay deep in the interiors of sunken ships. Once brought up, the bodies of dead sailors had to be identified and returned to grieving families, and salvage had to be cleaned and repaired.

Eventually, all but three of the sunken or damaged ships were repaired. The three that could not be salvaged were the USS *Arizona* and the USS *Utah*, which were too badly damaged to raise, and the USS *Oklahoma*, which was raised but considered to be too old to warrant repair.

Before any of this work could be completed, however, and before a full assessment of the attack on Pearl Harbor could be made, there was a much more immediate problem to face. Months of diplomatic efforts to avoid armed aggression had failed, and the subsequent secret assault on Pearl had been an outright act of war. The attack was a stunning shock to all of America—the military, government, and public alike. War was no longer just a possibility—it was a reality.

Chapter 4

The Aftermath

It was the early afternoon of December 7 when Secretary of War Henry Stimson called Roosevelt with the news. The president was having a working lunch with his chief foreign policy aide, Harry Hopkins. Roosevelt, shocked and solemn, immediately began drafting a speech to deliver to Congress.

As he worked into the evening, the president conferred with senior government and military officials. Among them were Marshall, Hull, Stimson, and Secretary of the Navy Frank Knox. An exception was Admiral Harold R. Stark, chief of naval operations, who was too busy dealing with the emergency to speak to Roosevelt even by telephone.

"It's No Joke"

Roosevelt also ordered public news bulletins. Although America had known for years of the potential for hostilities, for many the reality of outright war seemed far away. Less than a week before the attack, *Life* magazine had commented, "Americans do not even seem worried by the prospect of war."[49] But now a small country, thousands of miles away, had delivered a destructive blow on American-controlled soil. And so what should have been a typical day of rest became anything but typical. Writer Craig Shirley notes, "Sunday in America was . . . a day for church, for family meals, for reading the newspapers, listening to the radio, going for long walks, for afternoon naps, for working in the yard and visiting with neighbors."[50]

Beginning around 2:30 p.m. eastern time, the nation's four national radio networks broke into their regular programming to deliver incomplete, confused, and sometimes garbled bulletins. Virtually every American with access to a radio was riveted to one. Neighbors came running if they did not have their own radios. Managers of movie theaters interrupted Sunday matinees, stopping the films and walking onstage to deliver the news. One of the first direct reports the public heard came soon after the attack, when a reporter in Honolulu delivered an eyewitness broadcast for the NBC network. He climbed to the roof of the *Honolulu Advertiser* newspaper building with a microphone, surveyed the damage, and told the nation, "It's no joke, it's a real war."[51]

Roosevelt's Speech to Congress

The next day, December 8, Roosevelt delivered his speech before Congress. Millions of people—the largest radio audience up to that time in US history—listened to his somber words as they gathered at home or on city streets, where the speech blared from radio stores or improvised public address systems. Shirley writes, "[The] speech was broadcast live on every imaginable radio network, filmed and photographed by every imaginable news agency."[52]

The president spoke movingly of the tragedy and of the dangers that America faced. But he also underscored his confidence that the nation could meet the challenge:

> No matter how long it may take us to overcome this premeditated invasion, the American people, in their righteous might, will win through to absolute victory. I believe that I interpret the will of the Congress and of the people when I assert that we will not only defend ourselves to the uttermost but will make it very certain that this form of treachery shall never again endanger us.[53]

Roosevelt then formally asked Congress, as the president is required to do, for permission to declare war. The response was overwhelmingly positive. Both the Senate and the House of Representatives voted almost unanimously in favor of the president's request. Montana representative Jeanette Rankin, a staunch pacifist, cast the only dissenting vote. The *Wall Street Journal* of December 9 commented, "Hardly had the echoes of the President's address died away before the Senate passed a war resolution. The House acted less quickly only because of the greater length of time required to call the roll."[54]

As America declared war on Japan, the question of doing the same on the other Axis powers was still uncertain. The issue was settled on December 11 when Germany and Italy, in support of their Axis partner Japan, declared war on the United States. Roosevelt again asked for and received overwhelming support for permission to declare war in return, and America formally entered the European battle. Germany's dictator, Adolf Hitler, stated, "The fact that the Japanese Government, which has been negotiating for years with this man [Roosevelt], has at last become tired of being mocked by him in such an unworthy way, fills us all, the German people, and all other decent people in the world, with deep satisfaction."[55]

Isolationism Collapses

Since the 1930s Roosevelt had known that conflict with Hitler and the other Axis leaders was a strong possibility. However, American involvement in a war had until now met with resistance from isolationists—that is, those who opposed American intervention in foreign conflicts. Providing assistance to the Allies in the form of economic aid, which the United States was already doing, was one thing. Sending a generation of Americans to fight in a far-off war—especially to serve what was widely seen as other nations' interests—was another.

Before Pearl Harbor, a majority of Americans had been sympathetic to isolationism. Polls indicated that about 80 percent of the public approved of a hands-off approach, and most members of Congress shared that sentiment. Roosevelt would have had a difficult, if not impossible, task in convincing America to join the war. In his 1948 look back, Sherman Miles commented, "How the isolationist elements in the country . . . would have howled [before Pearl Harbor]! American lives to be sacrificed in defense of British and Dutch colonies, and Siam [Thailand]!"[56]

President Franklin D. Roosevelt signs the Joint Congressional Resolution officially declaring a state of war between the United States and Japan. Although one representative dissented, Congress quickly granted Roosevelt's request for a declaration of war.

All of that changed after the direct attack on American territory. Congress's overwhelming vote of confidence was one clear sign of this. Another was that isolationist groups, such as the influential America First Committee, dissolved. Even the famous aviator Charles Lindbergh, America's most prominent isolationist and a Nazi sympathizer, fell in line. When America entered the war, Lindbergh tried to renew his status as an officer in the air corps reserves. The Roosevelt administration, which was no friend to Lindbergh, refused to grant his request.

"A Date Which Will Live in Infamy"

President Franklin D. Roosevelt's speech before Congress, broadcast to the nation live on December 8, 1941, formally asked for permission to declare a state of war. Roosevelt's eloquent speech has become one of the most famous in American history. He said, in part:

> Yesterday, December 7th, 1941—a date which will live in infamy—the United States of America was suddenly and deliberately attacked by naval and air forces of the Empire of Japan. . . .
>
> It will be recorded that the distance of Hawaii from Japan makes it obvious that the attack was deliberately planned many days or even weeks ago. During the intervening time the Japanese Government has deliberately sought to deceive the United States by false statements and expressions of hope for continued peace. . . .
>
> Japan has . . . undertaken a surprise offensive extending throughout the Pacific area. The facts of yesterday speak for themselves. The people of the United States have already formed their opinions and well understand the implications to the very life and safety of our nation. . . .
>
> Always will be remembered the character of the onslaught against us. No matter how long it may take us to overcome this premeditated invasion, the American people in their righteous might will win through to absolute victory. I believe I interpret the will of the Congress and of the people when I assert that we will not only defend ourselves to the uttermost but will make very certain that this form of treachery shall never endanger us again. . . .With confidence in our armed forces, with the unbounding determination of our people, we will gain the inevitable triumph—so help us God.

Franklin Delano Roosevelt, "Pearl Harbor Address to the Nation," American Rhetoric. www .americanrhetoric.com.

Americans Sign On

With the collapse of isolationism came a vast outpouring of public approval for joining the battle. An editorial in the *New York Times* about Roosevelt's speech asserted, "The United States went to war today as a great nation should—with simplicity, dignity, and unprecedented unity. The deep divisions which marked the country's entrance into the wars of 1776, 1812, 1861, 1898 and 1917 were absent. Overnight, partisan, personal and sectional differences were shelved."[57]

In large part the American public's approval was fueled by a barrage of grim reports it heard on the radio and saw in newspapers and movie newsreels, especially in the form of chilling photographs and film footage of the attack on Pearl Harbor. These reports helped inspire, among other things, a flood of volunteers who wanted to join the armed forces. Within days, recruiting stations were staying open twenty-four hours a day to accommodate the hundreds of thousands of men (and a smaller number of women) who wanted to enlist.

Some of these volunteers, who had been aware that war was a strong possibility, simply stopped what they were doing at the moment they heard the news to hurry to the recruiters. Underage youth lied about their date of birth in order to be accepted by recruiters. Those who were rejected on medical grounds were crushed, and those who chose not to fight were mocked as unpatriotic. The *Washington Evening Star* reported, "Young boys of 'teen age' and grizzled veterans of the last war swamped Army, Navy and Marine recruiting stations today, ready to give their lives if necessary to whip [the] Japanese."[58]

The Impact of America's Entry

The events at Pearl Harbor, and the subsequent outpouring of support from volunteers and the government, had an immediate and decisive effect on the war. The Allied and Axis powers in Europe had been engaged in a full-scale conflict since 1939, and at the time of the Pearl Harbor attack the outlook was grim for the Allies. At this point Hitler controlled an empire larger than that of Napoleon, whose vast realm had spread across much of Europe in the late eighteenth and early nineteenth centuries. The Nazi-controlled regions now stretched from the Channel Islands in the English Channel east to Poland, and from Scandinavia in the north to Greece and the Balkans in the south. Hitler aimed to stretch this empire even farther, notably by waging attacks on the United Kingdom, North Africa, and the Soviet Union. His plan included not only outright warfare but also terrifying atrocities, particularly the program now called the Holocaust—the systematic imprisonment and murder of millions of Jews and other minorities.

US entry into the war after Pearl Harbor was a vital turning point in Germany's advance on all of Europe. Many historians feel that the Allies would likely have fallen to Germany if the United States had not begun fighting directly. The same was true with Japan's advance across the Pacific. But these advances were not successful. Following America's declaration of war, the battle became truly global, merging two widely separated battles—in the Pacific and Europe—into a single world war. By the time it was over, World War II had become by far the most extensive conflict in history, responsible for an estimated 60 million casualties.

America on the European Front

Once America's reluctance to join the battle faded in the wake of Japan's sneak attack, it wholeheartedly added its resources to aid the Allies. First and foremost were the human resources the United States could provide: that is, American soldiers. Millions of soldiers were sent to those regions of Europe that were not under Nazi control. At the same time, America's defense industry began turning out essential war matériel, such as planes, tanks, and weapons, at a furious pace. America was in a position to produce these tools of war much more quickly than the other Allied nations, largely because the war was not fought on US soil and so US factories had escaped destruction by enemy forces.

From the beginning of the conflict, even before Pearl Harbor, Allied leaders—in particular, Roosevelt and British prime minister Winston Churchill—had decided that the bulk of their resources should be directed first to the European theater. In part their reasoning was that Japan was still bogged down by its war in China and had fewer available resources, so it presented less of a threat than Germany. Although Japan was obviously a powerful enemy, the Allied leaders determined that it could be contained, primarily by American forces in the Pacific.

The United States thus took on the bulk of the fighting in the Pacific, but America's entry in the war boosted the Allies' capabilities in Europe as well. The United States cooperated closely in European action with the two main Allied nations that had not yet fallen to the Nazis: the United Kingdom and the Soviet Union. This cooperative effort took place on many fronts. For example, American bombers and fighter planes used air bases in England as stations for launching bombing raids on Germany, targeting such installations as transportation hubs, munitions factories, and synthetic oil plants. US entry into the war also meant that it could play a direct role in such Allied maneuvers as the invasions of Italy, Italian-held North Africa, and France.

Bestriding Asia

In the Pacific, meanwhile, the first shots of the war had begun within hours of the Pearl Harbor attack, and, at first, Japan seemed to be winning. Its ability to rapidly invade and occupy vast portions of the Pacific was in many ways as stunningly successful as the surprise assault on Pearl Harbor had been.

As a result, its Co-Prosperity Sphere soon encompassed parts of China as well as the Philippines, Malaya, French Indochina, the Dutch East Indies, Burma, a portion of India, and many Pacific islands. For about a year the Japanese even occupied the remote island of Attu in the Aleutian Islands off Alaska. John W. Dower writes, "At the peak of its expansion . . . Japan bestrode Asia like a colossus, one foot planted in the mid-Pacific, the other deep in the interior of China, its ambitious grasp reaching north to the Aleutian Islands and south to the Western colonial enclaves of Southeast Asia."[59]

The End Nears

For a time, it appeared that the Axis powers would be as unstoppable in Europe as they appeared to be in the Pacific. As the Japanese continued to solidify their control of Asia, Germany was having similar victories in its brutal invasion of much of Europe. For some six months, from the end of 1941 through mid-1942, there was a strong possibility that the Axis powers would succeed in both theaters. But then the Allied forces began to take the upper hand in both. For example, the Soviets halted Nazi progress toward Moscow in the Battle of Stalingrad, which lasted from August 1942 into early 1943. Another stunning victory was the Battle of the Bulge, fought in France, Belgium, and Luxembourg from late December 1944 into January 1945. Furthermore, the United Kingdom was able to resist extensive German bombing campaigns, particularly on the capital city of London. The Allies scored many other significant victories as well, notably the invasion of Normandy (D-Day) in June 1944. The tide was turning.

US troops go ashore at Normandy on June 6, 1944. The landing, part of an all-out Allied assault on northern France, marked the beginning of a sweep through Europe that ultimately led to the defeat of Nazi Germany.

In the Pacific, meanwhile, the Allies were similarly taking the upper hand. One crucial point came in June 1942, when both sides sought to occupy tiny Midway Island. The United States launched a surprise attack there that seriously crippled Japan's navy, just as the Japanese had done to the American fleet at Pearl Harbor. Another significant battle in the Pacific theater was the Battle of Leyte Gulf in 1944. It was the largest naval battle of World War II and perhaps the largest of its kind in history. Fought in the waters off Leyte, one of the islands in the Philippines, this conflict was part of a strategy to cut off Japan from its colonies elsewhere in Asia, thus blocking the flow of oil and other raw materials. (The Battle of Leyte Gulf also marked the first instance of organized attacks by Japanese *kamikaze* aircraft. This infamous strategy involved suicide missions in which pilots deliberately sacrificed themselves by steering their planes into their targets.) The conflict delivered a further devastating blow to the Imperial Japanese Navy's power and put an end to Japan's attempts to consolidate its control of the Philippines. By early-1945, the Allies were clearly winning in both the Pacific and European theaters.

Casualties on both sides were high. In five weeks of heavy fighting to control just the tiny island of Iwo Jima, for example, American forces sustained about 6,800 deaths and more than 19,000 wounded. The casualties on the Japanese side of this battle were even greater. Of the 21,000 Japanese troops on Iwo Jima, some 20,000 were killed and 1,000 taken prisoner. (The startlingly high number of Japan's casualties was because its soldiers typically fought to the death, surrendering only rarely.)

The End

As it became clear that America was winning the Pacific war, the United States drew up plans with the other Allied nations to invade not just Axis-held territory but the twin hearts of the enemy—Japan and Germany themselves. But this proved unnecessary. In Europe the Germans were in fast retreat, and Hitler realized that all was lost. He committed suicide in late April 1945, and by the beginning of May all of the German forces in Europe had surrendered. The Pacific theater continued to see battle into the summer of 1945. However, the Japanese were also in retreat, and the plans that the United States had drawn up to force a surrender—by invading Japan itself—proved to be unnecessary. This was because America dropped the most devastating weapon the world had yet seen—the atomic bomb—on its enemy.

The first use of an atomic bomb in combat took place on August 6, 1945. This one bomb almost completely destroyed the city of Hiroshima in central Japan, leveling 90 percent of the urban center and causing at least seventy thousand immediate deaths. Hundreds of thousands more were severely injured, missing, or sickened, including an estimated seventy thousand who died of burns or radiation poisoning within five years. Three days later, on August 9, another bomb leveled the southern city of Nagasaki, causing an estimated sixty-five thousand immediate deaths and leaving at least sixty-five thousand more sickened, wounded, or missing.

It became clear that Japan, already in retreat, would be unable to continue the battle. There was also another reason for Japan to give up the fight: The Soviet Union, which had until then remained neutral in the Pacific, declared war on Japan. On August 9 it attacked Manchukuo (Manchuria), Japan's last source of natural resources, in a move to acquire those resources for itself. Reporter Gareth Cook comments, "In that instant, Japan's strategy was ruined."[60]

The Surrender

Less than a week later, on August 15, Hirohito made a recording, which was broadcast to his nation, announcing Japan's surrender. In his heartfelt statement the emperor said, "I swallow my tears and give my sanction to the proposal to accept the Allied proclamation [of victory]."[61] As Hirohito's subjects listened, they were as stunned as Americans had been when Roosevelt spoke about Pearl Harbor. After years of official assurances that victory was inevitable, their expectations were shattered.

The formal surrender ceremony took place on September 2 aboard the battleship *Missouri*. In his speech General of the Army Douglas

A Japanese pilot on a suicide mission dives at a US warship in the Pacific in June 1945. The first instance of organized attacks by kamikaze pilots took place during the Battle of Leyte Gulf in 1944.

MacArthur, who had been a leading figure in the Pacific war, expressed his hope that "a better world shall emerge out of the blood and carnage of the past—a world founded upon faith and understanding—a world dedicated to the dignity of man and the fulfillment of his most cherished wish—for freedom, tolerance and justice."[62]

Since Germany and Italy had surrendered in May, Japan's capitulation meant that World War II was finally over. Not surprisingly, an immediate outpouring of joy and relief swept the nations of the Allied forces. The years of grief, sacrifice, and uncertainty were at an end. At the same time, the citizens of the conquered nations were stunned by their loss—but also experienced a range of complex emotions. A striking example of this

The Home Front

In addition to the destruction and loss of life in battle, World War II had a dramatic impact on daily life on the home front—that is, everyday citizens. In Nazi-occupied countries such as France and Netherlands, for instance, there was the very real element of danger. Anyone defying the German forces risked imprisonment or worse. Thousands of people, particularly Jews, went into hiding to avoid deportation to concentration camps.

Other aspects of the home front were dangerous, if somewhat less dire. In the United Kingdom, for instance, blackouts were ordered to foil German bombing raids. Citizens joined patrols to watch for enemy aircraft or made clothing for soldiers. And as a safety precaution, about 1.5 million English citizens, primarily children, were evacuated from urban areas to the countryside.

In all of the countries affected by the war, rationing was established. Items such as tires and gasoline became scarce, since materials such as rubber, leather, plastics, oil, and metal were needed for the war effort. Perhaps the biggest impact on the home front was a severe restriction on food, since it was needed for soldiers overseas. Sugar, meat, coffee, eggs, cheese, jam, butter, and a great many other items were in short supply or completely unobtainable.

These changes in lifestyle were severe, but they also fostered a strong sense of camaraderie and patriotism. A wide variety of public service ads, shows, posters, and pamphlets urged citizens to do their part for the war effort. In the United Kingdom, for example, patriotic mottoes like "There Will Always Be an England" were extremely popular.

was the reaction of the people of Japan. Many were simply devastated—a reaction symbolized by the crowd that gathered around the Imperial Palace in Tokyo, weeping and apologizing to the emperor for failing him.

The Course of History

US entry into the war dramatically altered world history. A confrontation previously confined to European nations battling for control of Europe became something quite different. The surprise attack on Pearl Harbor, and America's response to it, created a new theater of war—one that spanned the Pacific. A regional war became a truly global conflict. If not for the sneak attack on Pearl Harbor, the outcome of the war might have been radically different. It may well have ended in victory for the once-mighty Axis powers. Instead, the swift American response became perhaps the single most important element in the Allies' triumph. But now the war was over, and it was time to begin assessing the war's legacies—legacies that would be felt for decades to come.

Chapter 5

What Is the Legacy of the Pearl Harbor Attack?

After the surrender of the Axis powers, the combined state of affairs in Europe and the Pacific changed radically. Those nations that had been occupied by Axis forces were liberated by the Allies and began the slow, difficult process of rebuilding. France, for example, had been occupied by the Nazis and had been the site of especially heavy fighting. Millions of people had died or were seriously wounded. The nation's infrastructure and manufacturing capabilities were shattered, and in some cases entire towns and villages were destroyed. Its formerly strong colonial structure (especially in Africa and Southeast Asia) was shaky and eventually dissolved. Years of rebuilding lay ahead.

Meanwhile, the Axis powers experienced something that conquered people have experienced since the beginning of history: occupation by the victors. In Europe, Germany and Italy were occupied and controlled by a coalition of the Allied nations. However, the occupations in Europe were relatively brief compared with that of Japan. The Allied occupation of Germany and Italy lasted only about four years. On the other hand, America continued to occupy Japan for nearly seven years, until the spring of 1952.

The American occupation of Japan began in late August 1945, when Douglas MacArthur brought a team of military and governmental authorities into the country. He established a base of operations in Tokyo and imposed martial law on the entire nation. No Japanese person was allowed to travel abroad without express permission of the US forces. No major political, administrative, or economic decisions were possible without America's approval. No public criticisms of MacArthur or his regime were allowed (although dissident opinions were informally voiced).

During these years, American forces made significant efforts to rebuild the country. Many were successful, but the period was still one of hardship and shattered morale for the Japanese. Even earlier, during the war, Japan's home front had experienced adversity far worse than had taken place in the United States. Maintaining a decent life for civilians had never been a high priority for Japan's leaders, and there had been only sporadic, poorly developed plans for creating such projects and plans as public air raid shelters and the evacuation of citizens from cities that were potential targets.

Also, food supplies had been dangerously low in Japan during the war years. One reason for this was the need to feed soldiers overseas, which drained civilian resources. Another was a near absence of imported food, since embargoes cut off the island nation from outside sources. Vast acres of farmland lay ruined by repeated Allied bombing raids, and a major source of food—fishing—dropped to virtually nothing because civilian fishing fleets could not work in regions affected by the war. Widespread malnutrition resulted in Japan, and the looting of food supplies made up about half of all crimes in some areas. John W. Dower notes, "By 1944 theft of produce still in the fields led police to speak of a new class of 'vegetable thieves' and the new crime of 'field vandalizing.'"[63]

The lack of food and other resources, such as medicine and manufactured goods, led to further serious social problems, such as widespread poverty, prostitution, millions of homeless people living in crude shantytowns, and the rise of organized crime. These problems continued to plague Japan during the postwar years of US occupation, at least to a degree, aggravated by other severe issues such as the increased strain on resources caused by millions of Japanese returning from former colonies. Serious health hazards caused by ruined infrastructures such as

Japanese women and children wait in line for food rations in September 1945, one month after Japan's defeat and surrender. As part of the rebuilding of Japan, US occupation forces distributed food to millions of Japanese citizens who were threatened by starvation.

sewer systems and dangerously damaged building sites added still further complications.

One of the saddest aspects of postwar Japan was its shattered morale. For centuries the Japanese had recognized their emperor as a semidivine ruler, and they had fully accepted his assertion that their nation was predestined for glory. At the end of the war, however, they realized that their royal leader was, in fact, a fallible human and that he was not destined to lead them to victory. However, during the years of occupation, a determination to rebuild their shattered nation slowly began to surface. Dower writes,

Virtually all that would take place in the several years that followed unfolded against this background of crushing defeat. Despair took root and flourished in such a milieu [setting]; so did cynicism and opportunism—as well as marvelous expressions of resilience, creativity, and idealism of a sort possible only among people who have seen an old world destroyed and are being forced to imagine a new one.[64]

Rebuilding a Defeated Nation

MacArthur and the people under his command began their work amid this confusion and chaos. The general's plans for the occupation of Japan had several primary goals. One was to literally rebuild the country, creating new infrastructure through programs to repair or fashion roads, buildings, waste systems, and other structures. Another was to provide immediate help with food and other material aid. For example, during a disastrous harvest season in 1945, American food shipments kept an estimated 10 million Japanese from starvation.

But there was another, broader goal: the introduction of social change to Japan. MacArthur was determined to alter the basic structure of Japanese politics and, by extension, daily life by establishing a system of democracy and making other fundamental changes to the nation's political and governmental structure. Among other goals, the American occupying forces hoped to transform the Japanese view of themselves as subjects of an absolute ruler to citizens of a republic. To this end, MacArthur and his administration instigated a number of fundamental, groundbreaking, and widespread changes. Bill Gordon, a scholar of Japanese studies, comments, "The Allied Occupation of Japan occupies a unique place in the history of the world, being the only time [to date] an occupying force tried to democratize another nation by instituting sweeping political, social, and economic reforms."[65]

The most important of these reforms was the drafting of a new constitution. One crucial part of this new document laid the groundwork for the creation of a national democracy. It specifically stipulated that the emperor was no longer a supreme and semidivine leader; instead, he became a figurehead with only ceremonial power. A democratically elected government would now hold the nation's real political power.

Other reforms enacted during this period were inspired by the constitutions and laws of American and European nations. Among these were the recognition of fundamental human and civil rights, the creation of unionized labor, education and economic reforms, separation of church and state, the right to a fair trial in court, and women's right to vote. A program of land reform was also established, allowing farmers to own land instead of renting from aristocratic landowners. At the same time, some changes made during this period were on a smaller, grassroots scale. For example, teams of Americans across the country taught the basics of American-style civics to adults and schoolchildren.

Another key part of the new constitution was the so-called peace clause. The wording of this clause went far beyond simply condemning any future act of war. It stated that Japan now aspired to maintain an international peace based on justice and order and to renounce the waging of war as a means of settling international disputes. To this end, the new constitution specifically forbade Japan from maintaining land, sea, or air forces or any other organization that could potentially lead to armed conflict.

Generally, the shocked and disillusioned people of Japan accepted the governmental changes brought by the new constitution, and they welcomed the physical and concrete changes (such as new roads) built by the occupying American forces. Overall, in the eyes of many observers, the occupation was a success despite such problems as instances of corruption in food distribution. In an essay for the Columbia University East Asian Curriculum Project, one scholar comments, "The success of the Occupation can be judged by the fact that [decades] later, Japan has not fought a war, is a close ally of the United States, and has not changed most of the important reforms made by the Occupation."[66]

The Race to Build the Atomic Bomb

One of the legacies of the war was the atomic bomb. In the decades since, atomic weaponry has dramatically shaped global politics, and the peaceful use of atomic energy has had a similar impact on the world. The bomb was developed first by American scientists—which would not have happened if the attack on Pearl Harbor had not triggered America's entry into the war.

For years scientists knew that the bomb was possible and that it would be so powerful that the first nation to develop it would win the war. Germany, Japan, and America raced to reach that goal. Japanese and German scientists had been working on it since the mid-1930s, while the Americans began relatively late (in 1942). However, the Americans had an edge: They had the world's top scientists, in particular the brilliant physicist Albert Einstein. Einstein never worked directly on the bomb but is intimately associated with it. His work in theoretical physics was crucial to its development, and his urgent advice to Roosevelt about the danger of Germany creating the weapon helped spur America's commitment to the project.

When in 1943 the Allies destroyed Germany's plant for creating heavy water (a form of water needed for nuclear weapons), Japan and the United States became the only contenders. It was close, but America won the race and ended the war with its nuclear destruction of Hiroshima and Nagasaki on August 6 and August 9, 1941.

Postwar Prosperity

During the postwar years, other parts of the world were also undergoing major changes. The badly destroyed nations of Europe began to rebuild their factories, their economies, their homes, and their lives. In time, thriving economies developed in Britain, France, and other Allied or formerly occupied nations. Postwar changes in Germany also led to development of a vibrant economy and, over time, a new role for that country among the world's nations.

The United States also experienced postwar economic prosperity. Gross national product (GNP) is the value of a nation's services and products for one year. America's GNP more than doubled during the war, from about $100 billion in 1940 to nearly $212 billion by 1945, and this boom lasted well into the postwar years.

One reason for this rise was that during the war millions of Americans had bought war bonds, investments that helped finance the war effort and guaranteed buyers a modest profit after it ended. As a result, much of the money people had earned during the war was in savings accounts afterward, and the increased spending of these savings fostered the nation's prosperity in the postwar years. Another reason was that America's factories and farmlands were untouched during the war, giving the nation a huge advantage over the devastated countries of Europe in producing manufactured goods and food.

Social Change

In addition to economic changes, there were also less tangible but equally important shifts in society. One of these was a dramatic boost in equality for women. During the war American women had continued to fill traditional roles such as homemakers, secretaries, or nurses, but many other women had aided the war effort in other, more direct ways. For example, about one thousand of them formed the Women Airforce Service Pilots. Their job was to fly new warplanes from factories to airfields, marking the first time American women were allowed to fly military craft.

Furthermore, the millions of women who had stepped into other traditionally male professions, such as factory work, paved the way for major changes. By the end of the war, the number of women in the labor pool had jumped by more than 50 percent. Many of them worked in factory jobs, such as building airplanes and tanks. Their crucial roles were symbolized by a now-famous poster that featured Rosie the Riveter, a fictional factory worker who became an icon for the power of this new workforce.

Rosie the Riveter (pictured) became a patriotic symbol for women who joined the workforce during World War II. Many of these women worked in factory jobs building airplanes and tanks. Despite these new roles, women continued to face inequality after the war.

Redrawing the Map

In the wake of World War II, world geography dramatically changed as the victors sought to gain territory previously controlled by the Axis powers. Some of these changes occurred in regions largely untouched by the war itself. For example, millions of Jews migrated to a new nation in the Middle East: Israel, which was created by the Allies specifically as a Jewish state. Taiwan, Manchuria, and other regions in Asia were returned to China, while many other Japanese territories became independent (such as Korea) or United Nations Trust areas under US administration. And in North Africa, the Axis-controlled nations of Ethiopia, Libya, and Somalia were occupied by the United Kingdom and eventually became independent.

In large part, however, the changes were in Europe, and they created two overall regions, the Western countries and the Communist Eastern bloc, separated by what became known as the Iron Curtain. For example, the previously Nazi-controlled nations of Estonia, Latvia, and Lithuania became part of the Soviet Union. The Soviets also took control of Nazi-held Romania, Poland, and Czechoslovakia. And, of course, the Allies took possession of Germany itself. The capital, Berlin, was divided between 1945 and 1949 into zones controlled by the four main powers of the time: the United States, the United Kingdom, France, and the Soviet Union. The rest of Germany was split in two: West Germany remained democratic, while East Germany was in the hands of the Soviet Union.

Rosie may have symbolized the surge in women entering the workforce during the war, but overall there was still rampant inequality. Women were typically paid less than their male counterparts, and men often did not want women working outside the home once the need for doing so was over. Many women chose to leave their wartime jobs once the conflict ended, and many were replaced by returning soldiers. However, millions more chose to stay.

To a lesser degree, similar changes for women took place in other nations that had been part of the conflict. For example, during the war, women in Britain and other Allied nations were conscripted for factory work and as members of antiaircraft teams to shoot down German planes and missiles. The role played by British women in cracking German codes was also a deeply significant part of the war effort. In the Soviet Union, women had taken on even larger roles during the war. They were conscripted directly into the military and fought with distinction, often on the front lines. These and other changes in women's roles helped establish norms for future generations, and in time, working outside the home became an unexceptional way of life for women.

Related to this change in gender equality was another lasting legacy of the war: a step forward in the fight for civil rights, especially for American racial and ethnic minorities. During the war, for example, American black men had been drafted at the same rate as whites, and they had received the same pay. However, they were only allowed to serve in segregated units such as the famed Tuskegee Airmen. It was not until 1948, several years after the war's end, that Harry S. Truman (who became president after Roosevelt's death in 1945) signed a law integrating the armed forces.

Also bolstering the slow progress toward integration in the United States was an increased presence of millions of African Americans in the workforce during the war years. This was supported by a federal law, passed in the early days of the conflict, barring companies with government contracts from discriminating on the basis of race, creed, color, or national origin. And so the war created a legacy of increased equality that led directly to far more powerful changes in American civil rights during the 1950s and 1960s.

Seeking an End to War

In addition to sweeping social, political, and physical changes, the postwar years witnessed other profound shifts around the globe. Arguably the most important of these was a newfound determination to learn from past mistakes and prevent another world conflict. Never again, it was hoped, would the world be plunged into a destructive and all-encompassing conflict like World War II. If anything was to be gained by the tragedy of the war, it was the hope of preventing any future conflict on a worldwide scale.

The possibility of preventing future conflict has become the purpose of a particular agency. This organization today stands as perhaps the war's most enduring legacy. It grew directly out of a desire to keep Japan—or any nation—from threatening the world again. This organization was, and is, the United Nations, a huge entity devoted to global peace and support for cultural and social treasures. At its heart are both a council made up of representatives from member nations and a smaller entity, the Security Council, which has five permanent members (the United States, the United Kingdom, Russia, France, and China) and ten other rotating members.

The United Nations' forerunner, the League of Nations, had been born in 1919 in the wake of World War I. Like the United Nations, its goal was to maintain global peace and prosperity. The league was able to mediate and contain a number of small, regional conflicts. It failed, however, largely because isolationist sentiments in the United States prevented that nation from joining. Furthermore, Germany (as the primary aggressor in the war) was not allowed to join. This meant that two key players in world politics did not take part in the league's activities. Also, the organization had no power to actively intervene in a conflict, only to issue verbal warnings or economic sanctions. Furthermore, the League of Nations' structure, although dominated by the United Kingdom and France, required the unanimous agreement of all the members, a structure that kept the league from coming to agreement and acting on larger issues. This limited power meant that the league was unable to stop World War II. The league was formally dissolved in 1946.

In the meantime, during the war Roosevelt and the British prime minister, Winston Churchill, held secret talks about creating another organization dedicated to peace. They created a draft document, the Atlantic Charter, outlining this new organization. In time a revised version of the document resulted in the drafting of a charter for what would become the United Nations. The following spring, in June 1945, representatives of fifty nations signed the United Nations Charter at a conference in San Francisco, and the organization formally came into existence later that year. (One nation, Poland, joined later than the others and brought the number of founding nations to fifty-one.) Hopes ran high for the new entity. Addressing the delegates, Truman stated, "At no time in history has there been a more necessary meeting than this one. . . . You members of this conference are to be architects of the better world. In your hands rests our future."[67]

The Cold War and the Atomic Age

The United Nations has been the single most important player in still another lasting and wide-ranging legacy of the war: major changes in global politics. The most significant of these changes concerned the testy relationship between the Soviet Union and the United States, which had emerged as the two dominant political and military forces in the postwar years. Allies during the conflict, these superpowers (and the nations associated with them) became bitter enemies after it ended. Their incompatible social and political philosophies—one Communist and Socialist, one democratic and capitalist—helped foster this deep mutual suspicion. Their distrust of one another led to the so-called Cold War, a period of tension that lasted, with varying degrees of intensity, from the end of World War II until the dissolution of the Soviet Union in 1991.

A significant part of Cold War strategy was the so-called arms race—a contest of rapidly escalating military buildups. In particular both sides sharply increased their military capabilities. They stockpiled nuclear weapons, which themselves were a direct legacy of the war. Related to this has been the threat of nuclear capability on the part of other nations, along with the possibility that terrorist groups might get nuclear weapons. This threat continues to dramatically affect global politics today.

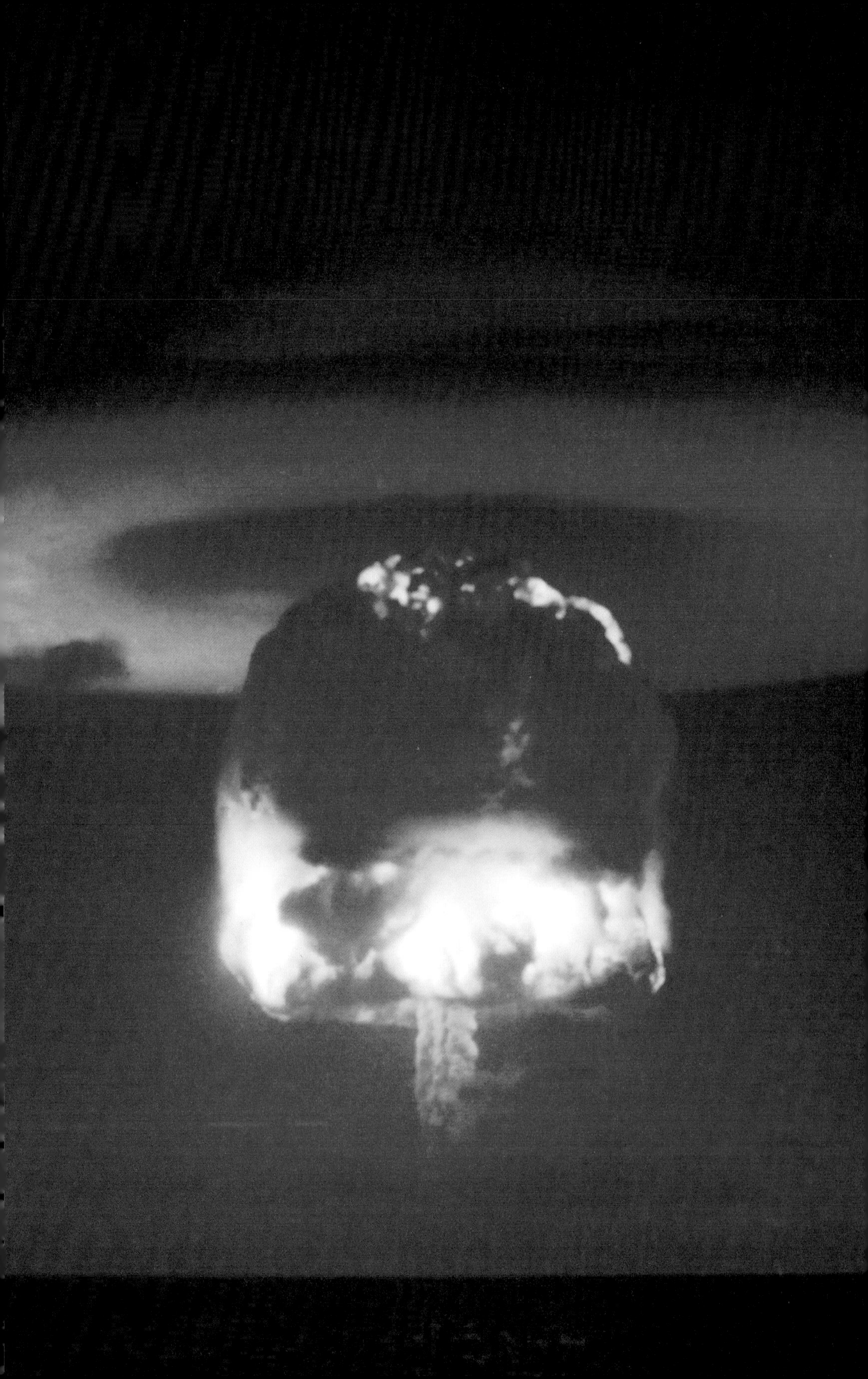

The United States detonates a thermonuclear weapon during testing in 1954. The development of nuclear weapons escalated during the Cold War, a lengthy period of tension between the United States and Soviet Union following World War II.

But weapons were not the only history-changing technology to develop in the atomic age, as the period of nuclear development has been called. Another aspect is the advance of atomic technology for peaceful purposes, such as nuclear power plants. This has had mixed results. Atomic power provides vast quantities of energy, but it is also extremely dangerous. This was tragically demonstrated by the nuclear power plant explosions and radiation poisoning resulting from the 2011 earthquake and tsunami in Fukushima, Japan. This catastrophe killed more than sixteen thousand people, with about another forty-five hundred missing and presumed dead. In addition, countless numbers of people have likely been subjected to deadly radiation poisoning as a result of the disaster.

The Former Axis Powers Snap Back

Although the United States and Soviet Union dominated world politics during the Cold War, within a few decades after the war many of the affected nations made huge strides toward reestablishing themselves internationally as well as domestically. In the case of Japan, for instance, this return to the world stage began in 1952, when the American occupation officially ended. (The United States still maintains a limited presence there in the form of military bases.) In the years since the end of the occupation, Japan's severe hardships have faded, replaced with a growing economy and revitalized public morale. Japan today ranks among the top economies in the world and is a leader in technological innovations, especially in electronics and automobiles.

Furthermore, Japan and its onetime bitter enemy, the United States, grew increasingly close in the years after the war. They became major trading and cultural partners again. Also, during the Cold War, America was interested in cultivating a close relationship with Japan for strategic military purposes, because both countries were threatened by Communist nations that were (and are) geographically near Japan: the Soviet Union, North Korea, and the People's Republic of China. For this purpose, the United States modified its previously imposed peace clause and pressured Japan to form its own Self-Defense Force. Historian W. Spencer Johnson writes, "The onset of the Cold War, and the confrontation with the Soviet Union, saw the United States and Japan share common concerns and shoulder common efforts to hold at bay a threat to both."[68]

Also, in the decades since the end of the occupation, the nations that once were the Axis powers have become increasingly important figures on the world political landscape. One example of this has been Germany's revival, especially following the 1990 merging of West Germany with Communist East Germany in the midst of the Soviet Union's collapse. Today reunified Germany has become the preeminent economic force in Europe and thus a major figure in world politics. Other significant moments in the advance of the former Axis powers had come before that: the admittance of all three to the United Nations. In 1955, ten years after the end of the war, Italy was granted membership. Japan gained membership in 1956. However, Germany was not granted the same status until 1973. In one sense, Japan may be considered a partial victor in the Pacific War. It was no longer responsible for maintaining a crushingly expensive military force, which had severely drained its money, resources, and manpower. Instead, it was able in the following decades to restore its reputation in the eyes of the world and to focus on rebuilding its economy, which it did with stunning success.

Remembering Pearl Harbor

Atomic energy, nuclear weapons, the Cold War, a desire for peace, and enduring changes in politics, economics, society, and cultures around the world—these are only some of the legacies created by the attack on Pearl Harbor and, by extension, World War II. More than half a century later, the wartime motto "Remember Pearl Harbor" is still relevant. This is powerfully symbolized by a moving memorial in Pearl Harbor, which honors the people who died on December 7. This memorial, which is today one of the most-visited places in Hawaii, is centered around the sunken remains of the USS *Arizona*—the ship that suffered the single most deadly catastrophe of the attack on Pearl Harbor. And so, more than half a century later, the "date which will live in infamy" continues to be a limitless subject of research and fascination—as well as a symbol of the ongoing struggle to achieve world peace.

Source Notes

Introduction: Pearl Harbor's Place in World History

1. Quoted in Franklin Delano Roosevelt, "Pearl Harbor Address to the Nation," American Rhetoric. www.americanrhetoric.com.
2. H.P. Willmott, *Pearl Harbor*. London: Cassell, 2001, p. 8.
3. Willmott, *Pearl Harbor*, p. 8.

Chapter One: What Led to the Attack on Pearl Harbor?

4. Quoted in William G. Beasley, *Japanese Imperialism, 1894–1945*. Oxford: Oxford University Press, 1987, p. 78.
5. Janis Mimura, "Japan's New Order and Greater East Asia Co-Prosperity Sphere: Planning for Empire," *Asia-Pacific Journal: Japan Focus*, December 5, 2011. www.japanfocus.org.
6. John W. Dower, *Embracing Defeat: Japan in the Wake of World War II*. New York: Norton, 1999, p. 21.
7. James Bowen, "Japan's Territorial Expansion in East Asia, 1875–1930," Pacific War Historical Society, May 14, 2010. www.pacificwar.org.au.
8. Quoted in BBC News, "Scarred by History: The Rape of Nanjing," April 11, 2005. http://news.bbc.co.uk/2/hi/223038.stm.
9. Quoted in Gordon W. Prange, *At Dawn We Slept*. New York: Penguin, 1982, p. 3.
10. Quoted in Trevor K. Plante, "Two Japans," *Prologue*, Summer 2001. www.usspanay.org.
11. Quoted in Plante, "Two Japans."
12. Quoted in Prange, *At Dawn We Slept*, p. 5.
13. Bowen, "Japan's Territorial Expansion in East Asia, 1875–1930."
14. Prange, *At Dawn We Slept*, p. 3.
15. Bill Gordon, "Greater East Asia Co-Prosperity Sphere," March 2000. http://wgordon.web.wesleyan.edu.

Chapter Two: The Buildup to War

16. Prange, *At Dawn We Slept*, p. 10.
17. Willmott, *Pearl Harbor*, p. 29.
18. Willmott, *Pearl Harbor*, p. 89.
19. Quoted in John Toland, *Infamy: Pearl Harbor and Its Aftermath*. New York: Doubleday, 1982, p. 254.
20. Toland, *Infamy*, p. 251.
21. Sherman Miles, "Pearl Harbor in Retrospect," *Atlantic*, July 1948. www.theatlantic.com.
22. US Army Center of Military History, "World War II Military Intelligence at the Center," September 10, 2011. www.history.army.mil.
23. Quoted in Pacific War Historical Society, "The United States Equips the Philippines to Resist a Japanese Attack." www.pacificwar.org.au.
24. Quoted in Craig Shirley, *December 1941*. Nashville: Thomas Nelson, 2011, p. 37.
25. Quoted in Vincent Ferraro, "Oral Statement on Indochina and the Oil Embargo Handed by the Japanese Ambassador (Nomura) to the Secretary of State on August 6, 1941," Mount Holyoke College. www.mtholyoke.edu.
26. Quoted in Vincent Ferraro, "Discussions with Japan 1941 and Pearl Harbor," Mount Holyoke College. www.mtholyoke.edu.
27. Quoted in Vincent Ferraro, "Draft Proposal Handed by the Japanese Ambassador (Nomura) to the Secretary of State on September 6, 1941," Mount Holyoke College. www.mtholyoke.edu.
28. Quoted in Ferraro, "Discussions with Japan 1941 and Pearl Harbor."
29. Quoted in Ferraro, "Discussions with Japan 1941 and Pearl Harbor."
30. Quoted in Ferraro, "Discussions with Japan 1941 and Pearl Harbor."
31. Quoted in Ferraro, "Discussions with Japan 1941 and Pearl Harbor."
32. Quoted in Avalon Project, Yale Law School, "Japanese Note to the United States, December 7, 1941," 2008. http://avalon.law.yale.edu.

Chapter Three: The Attack

33. Quoted in Prange, *At Dawn We Slept*, p. 427.
34. Quoted in "Memories of Hiroshima and Nagasaki," *Asahi Shimbun*, 2010. www.asahi.com/hibakusha/english/hiroshima/h02-00029-2e.html.

35. Quoted in Howard W. French, "Pearl Harbor Truly a Sneak Attack, Papers Show," *New York Times*, December 9, 1999. www.nytimes.com.
36. Quoted in French, "Pearl Harbor Truly a Sneak Attack, Papers Show."
37. French, "Pearl Harbor Truly a Sneak Attack, Papers Show."
38. Quoted in *Milwaukee (WI) Journal*, "Marshall Lists Pearl Harbor Day Activities," December 7, 1945. http://news.google.com/newspapers?nid=1499&dat=19451207&id=gk4aAAAAIBAJ&sjid=5CQEAAAAIBAJ&pg=1613,2754418.
39. Quoted in Official Pearl Harbor Tour Site, "Why Was Pearl Harbor Attacked?," 2012. www.pearlharboroahu.com.
40. Miles, "Pearl Harbor in Retrospect."
41. Quoted in Richard Goldstein, "Kermit Tyler, Player of a Fateful, If Minor, Role in Pearl Harbor Attack, Dies at 96," *New York Times*, February 25, 2010. www.nytimes.com.
42. Goldstein, "Kermit Tyler, Player of a Fateful, If Minor, Role in Pearl Harbor Attack, Dies at 96."
43. Quoted in The Official Pearl Harbor Tour Site, "Why Was Pearl Harbor Attacked?"
44. Quoted in C. Peter Chen, "Attack on Pearl Harbor," WWII Database. http://ww2db.com.
45. Quoted in U.S. Congressional Joint Committee on Pearl Harbor Attack Hearings, "Congressional Investigation Pearl Harbor Attack," December 21, 1941. www.ibiblio.org.
46. Frank L. Kluckhorn, "Japan Wars on U.S. and Britain; Makes Sudden Attack on Hawaii; Heavy Fighting at Sea Reported," *New York Times*, December 8, 1941. www.nytimes.com.
47. Chen, "Attack on Pearl Harbor."
48. Quoted in David H. Lippman, "The 55th Anniversary of the 'Day of Infamy.'" World War II Plus 55. http://usswashington.com.

Chapter Four: The Aftermath

49. Quoted in Shirley, *December 1941*, p. 159.

50. Shirley, *December 1941*, p. 127.
51. Quoted in University of Missouri–Kansas City Special Collections, "'Day of Infamy'—December 7th, 1941." http://library.umkc.edu.
52. Shirley, *December 1941*, p. 167.
53. Quoted in Roosevelt, "Pearl Harbor Address to the Nation."
54. *Wall Street Journal*, "Day of Infamy," December 9, 1941. http://online.wsj.com.
55. Quoted in Douglas Brinkley, *The "New York Times" Living History: World War II, 1939–1942; The Axis Assault*. New York: MacMillan, 2003, p. 276.
56. Miles, "Pearl Harbor in Retrospect."
57. Quoted in Shirley, *December 1941*, p. 170.
58. Quoted in Shirley, *December 1941*, p. 171.
59. Dower, *Embracing Defeat*, p. 21.
60. Gareth Cook, "Why Did Japan Surrender?," *Boston Globe*, August 7, 2011. http://articles.boston.com.
61. Quoted in Robert Trumbull, "A Leader Who Took Japan to War, to Surrender, and Finally to Peace," *New York Times*, January 7, 1989. www.nytimes.com.
62. Quoted in John W. Dower, "Shattered Lives," *New York Times*, July 4, 1999. www.nytimes.com.

Chapter Five: What Is the Legacy of the Pearl Harbor Attack?

63. Dower, *Embracing Defeat*, p. 90.
64. Dower, "Shattered Lives."
65. Bill Gordon, "The Allied Occupation of Japan," May 2000. http://wgordon.web.
66. Columbia University, East Asian Curriculum Project, "The American Occupation of Japan, 1945–1952." http://afe.easia.columbia.edu.
67. Quoted in History Learning Site, "The United Nations." www.historylearningsite.co.uk/united_nations.htm.
68. Quoted in Willmott, *Pearl Harbor*, p. 182.

Important People in the Attack on Pearl Harbor

Mitsuo Fuchida: The Japanese naval officer and lead pilot in the attack on Pearl Harbor.

Hirohito: The emperor of Japan who led his country through the war.

Cordell Hull: The US secretary of state and chief diplomatic negotiator in the talks before the war.

Husband E. Kimmel: An admiral in the US Navy and commander of the US Pacific Fleet during the Pearl Harbor attack.

Douglas MacArthur: A US Army general, key American military leader in the Pacific, and director of the US occupation of Japan after the war.

Kichisaburo Nomura: The Japanese ambassador and chief diplomatic negotiator in the talks before the attack.

Franklin D. Roosevelt: As president of the United States from 1933 to 1945, he declared war on Japan after the attack on Pearl Harbor and served throughout nearly all of World War II.

Walter C. Short: US Army lieutenant general and commander of Hawaiian ground and air defenses during the Pearl Harbor attack.

Hideki Tojo: Japanese general and prime minister who led the military government in Japan that executed the attack.

Isoroku Yamamoto: The Japanese naval general who spearheaded the plans to attack Pearl Harbor.

For Further Research 

Books

Thomas B. Allen, *Remember Pearl Harbor: American and Japanese Survivors Tell Their Stories*. Washington, DC: National Geographic, 2007.

Michael Burgan, *The Attack on Pearl Harbor: U.S. Entry into World War II*. New York: Marshall Cavendish, 2011.

Robert Greenberger, *The Bataan Death March: World War II Prisoners in the Pacific*. North Mankato, MN: Compass Point, 2009.

David Haugen and Susan Musser, eds., *The Attack on Pearl Harbor: Perspectives on Modern World History*. Detroit: Greenhaven, 2011.

David Horner, *World War II: The Pacific*. New York: Rosen, 2010.

John F. Wukovits, *The Bombing of Pearl Harbor*. Detroit: Lucent, 2011.

Websites

America Declares War on Japan—President Roosevelt Speech (www.history.com/speeches/fdr-asks-congress-to-declare-war-on-japan#fdr-asks-congress-to-declare-war-on-japan). An audio version of President Roosevelt's historic speech before Congress, asking permission to declare a state of war.

Boeing Plant: Seattle Washington, Tom Philo Photography (www.taphilo.com/history/WWII/USAAF/Boeing/index.shtml). A fascinating look at how one defense factory (along with many others) on the West Coast was camouflaged to blend in with its neighborhood to foil enemy air attacks.

Pearl Harbor Raid, 7 December 1941: Overview and Special Image Selection, Naval History & Heritage Command (www.history.navy.mil/photos/events/wwii-pac/pearlhbr/pearlhbr.htm). This site contains many striking images of the day of the attack.

Pearl Harbor, Voices of World War II: Experiences from the Front and at Home (http://library.umkc.edu/spec-col/ww2/pearlharbor/ph-txt.htm). An extensive collection of recordings from the era, including speeches, newsreels, personal reminiscences, and popular patriotic songs.

World War II, National Museum of American History (http://americanhistory.si.edu/militaryhistory/exhibition/flash.html). An excellent source for photos of the era.

Index

Picture Credits

Cover: © Bettmann/Corbis
Maury Aaseng: 16, 48
AP Images: 12, 65, 70, 75
© Bettmann/Corbis: 21, 33, 51, 57
© Corbis: 45, 80
© Hulton-Deutsch Collection/Corbis: 62
© Michael T. Sedam/Corbis: 30
Thinkstock.com: 8, 9

About the Author 

Adam Woog has written many books for adults, teens, and children. He has a special interest in history and biography. When not writing, Woog teaches in a preschool. He and his wife live in Seattle, Washington and have a grown daughter.